JAMES REDFIELD

THE CELESTINE PROPHECY

The Making of the Movie

Narrative and Editing by
Monty Joynes

HR

HAMPTON ROADS
PUBLISHING COMPANY, INC.

We either fear that human culture is falling apart, or we can *hold the Vision* that we are *awakening*. Each of us must consciously choose between these two futures.

Cover design by Steve Amarillo
Cover art from *The Celestine Prophecy*, the movie

Hampton Roads Publishing Company, Inc.
1125 Stoney Ridge Road
Charlottesville, VA 22902

434-296-2772
fax: 434-296-5096
e-mail: hrpc@hrpub.com
www.hrpub.com

If you are unable to order this book from your local
bookseller, you may order directly from the publisher.
Call 1-800-766-8009, toll-free.

Library of Congress Cataloging-in-Publication Data

Redfield, James.
  The celestine prophecy : the making of the movie / James Redfield
and Monty Joynes.
     p. cm.
  Summary: "The Celestine Prophecy: The Making of the Movie captures
the inside story of adapting one of the best-selling spiritual novels
of all time to the big screen. The book features more than 150
full-color photographs taken on the set during filming and from the
film itself, and an introduction from screenwriter/producer James Redfield,
author of The Celestine Prophecy"—Provided by publisher.
 ISBN 1-57174-458-4 (9x11 tc : alk. paper)
1. Celestine prophecy Motion picture) I. Joynes, St. Leger. II. Title.
PN1997.2.C45R43 2005
791.43'72—dc22
                   2005013146

ISBN 1-57174-458-4

10 9 8 7 6 5 4 3 2 1

Printed on acid-free paper in China

Coquina

Here is a little piece of St. Augustine to take with you, a piece of coquina, a native stone from Anastasia Island used to build the Castillo 300+ years ago along with many other things. It is the stone with which Colonial St. Augustine was built.

We think it is a stone that says much about our city:

Coquina is a single stone made from millions of individual shells, not unlike our city's history, which has taken 438 years of individuals living day to day to bring us to where we are this day, this one town; and . . .

Coquina is a stone that at first appearance seems pliable, relaxed like the city, because it is easily mined from the earth and shaped for useful purposes, but when tested can prove its strength, capable of weathering the heat of battle and centuries of storms.

Keep coquina close, and you'll keep St. Augustine close.

Paul K. Williamson
Director of Public Affairs
City of St. Augustine, Florida
Feature film location for
The Celestine Prophecy

Contents

From Novel to Movie

*I*t is difficult now to comprehend the impact of *The Celestine Prophecy* when it appeared in the Warner Books hardback edition in March of 1994. The relatively short novel had originally been self-published in trade paperback in 1993; and James and Salle Redfield had taken the book personally to independent and alternative bookstores, primarily in the South, and literally given away half of the 3,000 copies in the first printing to anyone who would read it. Within months, the word of mouth on the book prompted re-order after re-order; and before Warner secured the publishing rights, the Redfields had sold more than 100,000 copies.

In 1995 and 1996, *The Celestine Prophecy* was the best-selling American book in the world. It stayed on the *New York Times* bestsellers list for over three years, was translated into more than 40 languages, and ultimately influenced the world with some 12 million copies in print. A 2000 *New York Times* Reader's Poll named *The Celestine Prophecy* as the #1 all-time bestseller in religion, spirituality, and philosophy.

From Toronto to Melbourne, New York to London, Cape Town to Jakarta, San Diego to Rio de Janeiro, and Chicago to Rome, there are more than one hundred cities worldwide where organized groups still gather to discuss the relevance of *The Celestine Prophecy* to their lives.

Since the worldwide phenomenon of *The Celestine Prophecy*, James Redfield has continued his authorship of visionary literature in some ten additional books and ten audiotapes. His wife and partner, Salle Merrill Redfield, has further contributed to their work with meditation books and tapes. *The Tenth Insight*, the second novel in the Celestine series, went to #2 on the *New York Times* bestseller list in 1996, and the third novel—*The Secret of Shambhala: In Search of the Eleventh Insight*—was published in November 1999. There are now more than 20 million James Redfield books in print in more than 50 foreign languages.

With all this unparalleled success of a single novel, it was certain that Hollywood producers would want the rights to turn *The Celestine Prophecy* into what—an action-adventure movie? Offers were made—multi-million-dollar offers that only required James Redfield to sign a contract—but his intuition led him not to accept them. He expressed his intention on his website: "We want this film to come into being in accordance with the vision of the new spiritual consciousness that the story seeks to describe."

In his development of *The Celestine Prophecy* movie, James reaffirmed his trust in synchronicity. From the process of writing a screenplay to his choices for co-producers, from location searches to casting, from filming to distribution, James Redfield remained faithful to the Celestine Insights. For everyone involved in the making of the movie, the Seventh Insight provided a template for behavior: "Discover that intuitive thoughts are there to guide us and once followed, increase the synchronicity that leads us toward the actualization of our contribution."

Any film is a collaborative effort, but the making of a movie that matters requires a conscious focus of intention from everyone involved. Acting and directing, for example, are a search for authentic moments captured on film. These moments transcend the distance between creation and experiencing, and they thus abolish the space and time between the images on the screen and the felt emotions of the audience. A good film does more than transport, however; it involves. To what degree it involves is a measure of its significance and its power to persist in time from generation to generation by remaining relevant and meaningful.

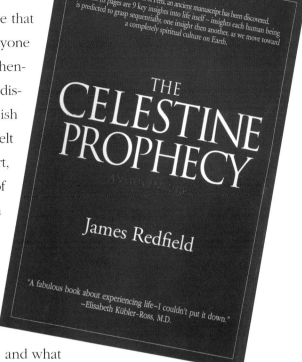

But before the collaboration that arises in the making of a movie, there is the vision of the writer. In the case of *The Celestine Prophecy: The Movie*, the vision of James Redfield was not compromised. His commitment to making spiritual truths accessible was evident throughout the cinematic journey, and what he once imagined can now be experienced on the big screen.

The Author's Vision
James Redfield

*T*he making of *The Celestine Prophecy* movie has been a long and interesting adventure, beginning years before the screenplay was written, or the actors signed, and even—believe it or not—before the book itself was conceived. In fact, if the truth be known, the book first dawned on me visually, as a series of images, dramatic scenes, that all arrived in my head feeling like movie moments.

Later, written up journal style, the book then came alive in a way, first for me, and then for many others. And while I could say it was based on my personal experience, I have never claimed much credit for what it became. The book was an adventure that I partly lived but mostly just received, and it somehow struck universal chords of the soul, first for me, and then apparently for almost anyone else, at any time, who wonders about the purpose of life at a deeper ontological level.

Turning it into a movie posed a certain dilemma, however. Images were one thing, but that many images, well, were unmanageable. Hollywood was adamant. Adaptation of this book couldn't be done. There were too many ideas, too many connections that existed at ever deeper levels of the subtext, too many long, winding dialogues that roamed here and there, only making sense in the last moments as the many drawstrings were pulled together. No way to get it clearly expressed in two hours, or even three. Perhaps a 16-hour miniseries, they said.

But as it turned out, even that genre seemed wrong, for other reasons. And so for years we hung in that particular no-man's-land between being sure we should do this film and yet having no idea how. Until at last, a certain realization set in. We had to face the fact that the film had to be a different kind of parable from the book, with a complicated but more global meaning, a kind of snapshot of the Celestine worldview that became ever more impactful with each subsequent viewing—but all laced within a story line that had a beginning, a middle, and an end, and moved along at a rate that moviegoers expect.

James and Salle with director Armand Mastroianni

So that's what we decided to do, or I should say, that's what we finally allowed to happen. In fits and starts, the synchronicity began to pour through, and in the end, everyone we needed showed up at just the right time: the investors, the crew, the cast, even the groups involved in the early tests of the movie.

All that's left now is for the real test to happen as this movie is released into the world. I would only ask that you remember one thing. The real impact is one you'll sense more fully without thinking. It will be something you feel—not so much with your emotions, but with your body, your soul—as a distantly familiar world begins to emerge. We can only hope that those same images—call them archetypes, clicks into a higher awareness—will do their thing again. And perhaps we'll now actually embrace a reality that before we could only intuit—a reality that's always been right here in front of our eyes, a glance away, in the sky, in the trees, in the light reflecting on a human face . . . just waiting until we had the eyes to see.

James Redfield
Producer and Co-Author of the Screenplay

James Redfield has been keenly interested in human spirituality all of his life. He grew up in a rural area near Birmingham, Alabama; and from an early age, he was motivated by a need for clarity about spiritual matters. Brought up in a Methodist church that was loving and community oriented, he was nevertheless frustrated by a lack of answers to his questions about the true nature of spiritual experience. As a young man, he studied Eastern philosophies, including Taoism and Zen, while majoring in sociology at Auburn University. He later received a master's degree in counseling and spent more than 15 years as a therapist to abused adolescents. During this time, he was drawn into the human potential movement and turned to it for theories about intuitions and psychic phenomena that would help his troubled clients.

Since 1994, when Warner Books published *The Celestine Prophecy* in hard cover, this adventure parable about a spiritual journey to Peru became one of modern publishing's greatest success stories. According to

Publishing Trends, The Celestine Prophecy was the #1 international bestseller of 1996 (#2 in 1995). In 1995 and 1996, it was the #1 American book in the world. This phenomenal novel spent over three years on the *New York Times* bestsellers list and appeared on lists around the world.

James Redfield also authored two more adventure tales in the Celestine series—*The Tenth Insight* and *The Secret of Shambhala*. In 2002, he also co-authored *God and the Evolving Universe* with Esalen founder Michael Murphy and filmmaker Sylvia Timbers.

James Redfield partnered with Barnet Bain in writing the screenplay for *The Celestine Prophecy* movie.

James with producer Barnet Bain

Barnet Bain
A Producer's Vision

*L*ife, yours and mine, is essentially a spiritual journey no matter what we see as our occupation or our duty. As a movie producer, I have discovered that we teach what we most need to learn. We hold up the mirror to ourselves by our choices and our designs, and we reveal who and what we are. *The Celestine Prophecy* holds up a mirror to reflect our potentials and possibilities, and it shows us the tools of our own empowerment so that we, as individuals and societies, can achieve our divine destinies.

Producing a film is a management process, but it can also be a conscious journey of magnificent proportions. Once one makes a commitment to leading a life of spiritual causality, the complex effort of filmmaking becomes, by its own nature, a spontaneous and synchronistic experience. The individual talents required for this significant collaborative activity present themselves, and the process thus becomes psychically inclusive. The harmony of all interactions is encouraged by the purpose itself, and those of us who give ourselves to it enjoy a great sense of being blessed.

Barnet and James in the producing mode

Barnet and Armand check out the props.

All that occurred in the making of *The Celestine Prophecy* movie was the result of a sacred intention to be faithful to its purpose. No individual was above this common goal. Each of us was linked in the fellowship of creation, and now, through the power of this medium, we are connected to you; and you, in very real terms, enter the creative process with us because it was our intention from the very beginning to serve you, to share with you the truth we most need to learn.

The truth is that we are not separate. As Thomas Jefferson wrote, we are endowed by our Creator "with certain unalienable Rights, that among these are Life, Liberty, and the pursuit of Happiness." Mr. Jefferson was speaking of the body politic in his *Declaration of Independence*, but the same is true in the metaphysical dimension. We have the right to freedom and joy, but in our cultural conditioning, perhaps we have lost the key to that fulfillment. What we require then are new insights to end our sense of separation so that we can reconnect to the divine energy that has always been our source and our strength.

The vision that I embrace is that we exist in a boundless universe of energy and that we are capable of loving relationships in each and every encounter if we make spiritual union our conscious intention.

The Celestine Prophecy, the movie, was thus intended as a vehicle to transport us all to the realization of our higher selves and our common human destiny.

Barnet Bain
Producer and Co-Author of the Screenplay

Producer and screenwriter, Barnet Bain has earned a reputation for creating innovative projects that celebrate the human spirit. His movies as producer include 1998's "life after death" Oscar winner *What Dreams May Come*. His recent television production *Homeless to Harvard: The Liz Murray Story*, a powerful celebration of the difference teachers can make in the lives of young people, received three Emmy nominations and earned him the Christopher Award as well as an Emmy Award nomination for Outstanding Made for Television Movie of 2003. He is the screenwriter of the Warner Bros. film *Jesus*, which continues to screen worldwide and has been translated, to date, into 848 languages. The *New York Times* (Sunday, February 8, 2004) noted the film may have become the most-watched movie ever. Other distinguished productions include *The Linda McCartney Story* and *Quantum Project*, the first Hollywood motion picture developed and produced specifically for the Internet. Barnet has produced a dozen motion pictures over the last decade.

Armand Mastroianni
The Director's Vision

*B*arnet Bain introduced me to *The Celestine Prophecy* project by bringing the script to a movie set where I was working. To demonstrate the synchronicity of our coming together, I had actually met Barnet to talk about making a movie in 1979 after I had completed my first feature film. Then, 20 years later, we collaborated on *The Linda McCartney Story* for CBS. Barnet was the executive producer, and I directed. Our professional relationship turned to friendship, and we both looked forward to a future project together.

Armand emulates rejoicing for a scene with Matthew Settle as John.

After I read the script that James Redfield and Barnet had crafted, I conceptualized the film as a love story—a story about falling in love with a philosophy. I didn't want the film to be stylized or gimmicky or to have any visual tricks in storytelling because I believed that the all-important Insights should have center stage. Seeing a film is not like reading a book. The audience can't stop the film to consider what has just been said, so clarity and pace are essential in relating *The Celestine Prophecy* while, at the same time, the flow must also be engaging and visually interesting. What appears on screen has to be relatable to the audience, and the dialog should never sound didactic.

When I met James, I experienced the clarity of his vision, and I wanted very much to collaborate in making the movie. I had read the book in the mid-90s myself, and I was aware of its popularity. I was also somewhat surprised that it had not been previously produced. There had been offers, to be sure, but James had honored his own philosophy in waiting patiently for all the elements and people to come together in a synchronous production event.

It was very, very helpful to sit with James and to carefully go through the script and understand all the Celestine moments—the pulse beats—that he felt were necessary to the storytelling, especially those insightful moments that his millions of readers were expecting to experience in the film. These direct insights into his creation became very important in a two-week rehearsal period that we don't usually get in films today. This time with the actors allowed us to involve them in the Celestine thought process. It was interesting that every cast member quickly embraced the Celestine ideals. They got it. And I think that every actor felt privileged to have James involved in this way. From the beginning, a very compassionate, healthy, and creative working environment was established.

In casting, we had to deal with all the relationship issues that are evident in the story. No single character could overshadow the others. They all had to evolve in a synchronistic way. I want to congratulate all our actors for turning in wonderful performances, and I want to thank them for being so open to the suggestions that were being made. Each one of them brought something unique to their film character.

Matthew Settle has the most crucial role because his character has the biggest arc. He starts off as a skeptic, and then he falls in love with the Celestine philosophy. His performance had to be tailored so that the audience could see that growth happening right up to the moment of

Armand working on the set with script supervisor Katie Waters

his epiphany when everything changes for him. Matthew is a very interesting and aggressive actor. I say "aggressive" in the sense that he challenges the material in a way that I like to encourage. I'm very proud of what came out of his work in his transition from skepticism to enlightenment.

Sarah Wayne Callies brings so much spontaneity to her performance, and those eyes—you can lose yourself in her eyes! I love the scene where she reveals the Eighth Insight to Matthew's character, and we see her pass from an intellectual knowing to profound understanding. We see the emotional acceptance on her face in the exact moment of discovery. Sarah Wayne is wonderful as she makes that instant totally real.

Annabeth Gish plays a character who has already made the journey of Sarah Wayne's character. She has so much information to impart. Annabeth's character, Julia, is quietly confident and centered in her view of the Insights as she shares them with the others. Annabeth is perfect in this role because she is such a gifted listener and reactor. Her great intelligence shines through in every scene.

We were lucky to get Thomas Kretschmann as Matthew's companion and guide throughout much of the film. The two actors had worked together before, so we were able to build on that relationship. Thomas has a kind of openness and inviting quality to his personality that he brought to his character, so the audience trusts him and believes him in the role of Wil. His empathy with Matthew's character in furthering John's courageous quest for the Insights is very well played.

In addition to Thomas, who is German, we were very fortunate to pull together others in an international cast, which I like because it gave the film a sense of universality. Joaquim De Almeida, for example, is Portuguese. He has played so many heavies in films that it was great to see him in the role of Father Sanchez because Joaquim is such an accessible, giving guy. In our film, he even provides some humorous relief. He has a motorcycle to tinker with, so he is not just another angel on the path to John's enlightenment.

I was in awe of Jürgen Prochnow's performances in *Das Boot* and other films. He proved to be very thoughtful in giving dimension to the character of Jensen, the film's antagonist. In the 1622 prologue sequence, Jürgen as the chief conquistador, without any lines, is magnificent. You can't keep your eyes off him in the scene. And wherever the character Jensen appears, Jürgen invests him with mystery and a subtly sinister foreboding.

Hector Elizondo is a dear friend. Early on, I gave him the option of playing the role of the Peruvian Cardinal Sebastian entirely in Spanish. He agreed, and there is only one scene—in the presence of the American character John—that he speaks English. Hector even translated my directions into Spanish for the benefit of the other actors, which speaks to his generous, caring nature. Hector is both an amazing person and an amazing actor.

Armand plans a shot with first assistant director Carl Ludwig.

In designing the look of the film with cinematographer Michael Givens, I wanted a wide-screen format to incorporate the scope of the Celestine subject and to allow for the peripheral vision that is our natural visual experience. Michael lobbied for a warm color palette, and we chose to use a digital internegative so that we could control and enhance the colors frame by frame. By this technique, we are able to stimulate the greens and the flowers of the natural environment to reflect what the characters were seeing in their heightened psychic states. Subtlety, however, was our conscious focus because we wanted to stay within the scope of reality.

I can't say enough about Barnet and Terry Collis, too, for their important and supportive friendship. Terry was essential in obtaining the equipment and crew necessary for a quality production. All the producers, including Beverly Camhe, created a comfortable environment for me to work in. I never felt the pressure of "We can't do this," which is usually the case during a tight shooting schedule.

James and Salle Redfield set the tone for the filmmaking process early on when they invited opinions and conversations that stimulated the creative process, and there was a unique harmony on the set inspired by their presence. Everybody—cast and crew—wanted to be there, and as a company, we paid attention to what was important. We were not distracted by what was extraneous, by those things usually motivated by ego.

Salle was an especially radiant presence in every phase of the moviemaking. Her inner light and strength contributed so much to those wonderful and innovative days.

My approach was always to broaden the audience, to include a new generation of moviegoers who had not read the book. I think that the adventure of the quest for the Celestine Insights brings that new audience along. The quest itself is also a metaphor for the often difficult and painful journey toward awareness and enlightenment that we all share.

I believe that our film of *The Celestine Prophecy* has been faithful to James Redfield's original vision and that its message will resonate with movie audiences all over the world. This is a film to be savored and discussed as something synchronous to the most important events of our time, both on a personal level as well as an international one. We all need a new perspective on the beautiful adventure of living. *The Celestine Prophecy* movie helps to open our eyes and hearts to the possibilities.

Armand Mastroianni
Director

Armand Mastroianni has been directing feature films and television for the past 25 years beginning with his first—*He Knows You're Alone*—which was released by MGM in 1980 and featured the screen debut of Tom Hanks. That film led to a long string of features including *The Killing Hour*, developed with William Friedkin, *The Supernaturals, Distortions, Cameron's Closet,* and *Double Revenge.*

In between shooting feature films, Armand Mastroianni began to direct television episodic programs, including *Dark Shadows, Against the Law, Friday the 13th, War of the Worlds, Reasonable Doubt, Touched by an Angel,* and *Dead Zone.*

Working almost non-stop, Armand has directed several highly received miniseries, including Danielle Steel's *The Ring* and Robin Cook's *Invasion*. His two-hour movies include *The Linda McCartney Story, Dare to Love,* Robin Cook's *Virus, Final Run, Deep Trouble, Nowhere to Land, Fatal Error, First Target, First Shot,* and for the TBS Superstation, *First Daughter,* which was the highest-rated movie for cable to date.

Prior to directing *The Celestine Prophecy,* he directed *Gone but Not Forgotten,* a four-hour miniseries starring Brooke Shields, Scott Glenn, and Lou Diamond Phillips based on the novel by Philip Margolin, for Hallmark Entertainment.

Since filming *The Celestine Prophecy,* Armand has directed two Jane Doe mystery movies for television—*Till Death Do Us Part* and *Now You See It, Now You Don't,* starring Lea Thompson and Joe Penny. His most recent project is directing a romantic comedy for the Hallmark Channel.

Armand directs Matthew Settle as John and Annabeth Gish as Julia in Washington Oaks.

Salle Redfield
Executive Producer

I remember the day James and I made a total commitment to making *The Celestine Prophecy* movie. It was a cool November afternoon in 2003, and we were in Sedona, Arizona, on a lecture tour. We were sitting in front of a fire talking about how making the movie would change our lives and require certain sacrifices. We always felt we wanted creative control when *The Celestine Prophecy* was made into a movie, but we knew the timing had to be right. And even though we had already opened a production office in Studio City the month prior, something about our fireside conversation solidified our commitment.

By that time, James and Barnet Bain had written the screenplay, much of it at our home in Birmingham, Alabama, and the production team was in place. Soon pre-production began in earnest. It did not take us long to realize that moviemaking is a 12-hours-a-day job, seven days a week. It is both exhilarating and exhausting, and it amazed us to see the daily accomplishments of a motivated team of movie professionals.

One of my favorite early experiences was the casting of the movie with Andrea Stone, C.S.A., a casting director with 25 years of experience in the film industry. Working with Andrea was almost magical at times because she shared our vision of the film, and she devoted herself to finding actors who could emotionally invest in that vision. It was not an easy job, and Andrea put a lot of prayer energy into the casting. I believe her intuitions were later rewarded on the movie set.

The location scouting was another phase that was a favorite. When we were making location decisions, and we went to St. Augustine, a very sweet coincidental memory surfaced in me. Years ago I was on vacation with my mother, and we drove down from Jacksonville to spend the day in St. Augustine. While there my mother told me there was a man she knew

in Birmingham whom she really wanted me to meet. The man, she said, went to her church, was very wise, and he was just the kind of man I said I always wanted to marry. That man turned out to be James. Thirteen years later he and I were there in St. Augustine, together, a full circle of fulfilling one of our most cherished dreams. It felt like the happiest form of cosmic humor and synchronicity.

Next came the actual production of the film, which happened to be one of the most creatively rewarding experiences I had known. I must have teared up with joy at least once a day for the first week. When the actors spoke their lines, James and I would look at each other in pure wonder at the reality of a dream coming to life. Even when one of the production assistants handed me a high-backed chair with *The Celestine Prophecy* on the back of the canvas, and my name on the front, my eyes misted once again.

Throughout production I was also impressed with the way each department, from production design, to wardrobe, to craft services, to camera operation, considered its work crucial to the success of the film. Everyone knew that in order for the actors to bring the script to life, everything else had to be in place. As for me, I felt my responsibility on the set was to uplift the cast and crew by the principle of the Eighth Insight. Instead of

Salle and James share a moment with Matthew Settle as John.

taking energy from them, I wanted to give energy. It was more of a silent role than anything. Everyone else had such an active position at that point. My function as an executive producer was mostly concentrated in the pre-production and post-production phases, so I was free to be on the set and watch the experience unfold.

After the long shooting day, we had daily film rushes to preview and discuss, plus we had our family and career lives going on at the same time. I had an article to write each month for our website newsletter, there were correspondences to answer, and we also had our workshop organization to manage. We didn't get much sleep, and we marveled at the stamina of the cast and crew. After working all day and half into the night, they wanted us to go out and play!

One person who helped us manage it all was our dear friend and associate John Austin. Sadly, he died unexpectedly at the age of 50 while we were still in post-production. John supported us on location with his unique talents, and he thoroughly enjoyed the filmmaking experience. Often he mentioned how grateful he was to be on location, and James and I will be forever thankful that we got to share the adventure with him.

Through the editing of the film, the movie became very personal to me. I would watch Maysie Hoy knit certain movie takes together, and I would have a memory of James and Barnet putting that scene down on paper. Often I would think back to the enormous challenge of adapting James's book into a movie. Being a part of the entire process was a privilege, even with my steep learning curve as a first-time producer.

Aside from its storytelling value, I believe *The Celestine Prophecy*, the movie, is a valuable teaching tool that carries the same uplifting energy as the book. I only hope that as people watch it, they also somehow feel the love, effort, commitment, and determination—on the part of many—that went into it. Besides that, I hope they walk away uplifted and seeing the world in a whole new way.

Salle Redfield
Holding the Center

She was there at the beginning when she fell in love with a psychologist who had the draft of a novel. She was there through the rewrites and then as wife and financial partner through the self-publishing and the showing of the book to alternative and independent bookstores. She held an abiding intuition that the book was important, and Salle Redfield then witnessed the international best-selling acceptance of it.

When Salle and James lecture together, Salle begins their programs with a guided meditation. Warner Books, now publisher of *The Celestine Prophecy*, saw Salle lead a meditation in 1995 and offered her a contract on what became an important resource for readers of the novel—*The Joy of Meditating*. Salle's writing also appears on www.celestinevision.com, *The Celestine Prophecy* website.

In the twelfth year of their partnership and marriage, the couple's intention to adapt *The Celestine Prophecy* into a wide-release movie was realized. Throughout the process,

from production agreements to casting to location searches, Salle was an integral part of the vision making. On the movie set, from first day to last, she appeared with James to hold the center of the consciousness of purpose for the film. And amid the demanding activity of actors and crew and equipment all around her, her radiant smile and confident intensity were both seen and felt. Although youthful, with sometimes tousled blonde hair, Salle Redfield stood as the gentle and protective Mother of the film's family, and she held the center of all good intentions to make *The Celestine Prophecy* movie a conscious reflection of her husband's life-changing book.

Terry Collis
Producer

Moviemaking is networking with creative and crafts people that you respect and trust. Barnet Bain invited me into the making of *The Celestine Prophecy* movie in its earliest stages and challenged me with a difficult location and a number of production problems. I read the script, but my involvement was crystallized when I spent time with James Redfield and understood the author's dedication to producing a film that was faithful to the book. Redfield was straightforward in his ability to communicate his vision. It was only then that I realized that I wanted to play a role in the making of *The Celestine Prophecy*.

The obvious options for locations that could equate to the mountainous Peruvian rainforest of the novel were Peru itself, Brazil, Mexico, Costa Rica, and Puerto Rico. I saw the far locations as a logistical nightmare and a stretch of resources. The scenery was appropriate, but moving an entire film company over a number of locations would be a hardship on all concerned. At that point in the location search, I suggested Florida, but no one else could see it. The validity of my research and intuition was proved in an abandoned Ocala limestone quarry, and again in the Washington Oaks rainforest, and finally in the Renaissance colonial architecture of St. Augustine. With the key decision on locations made, I assembled an incredible film crew that proved to have the same passion and dedication to realizing the vision that has become *The Celestine Prophecy* film.

Terry Collis
A Profile

Terry Collis is a veteran of more than 25 years in the motion picture industry. An early credit was as a stuntman on *Thelma and Louise.* He is now a successful filmmaker with extensive background as a producer and production manager of feature films and years of experience as a production executive for major Hollywood companies.

Terry at the Ruins set with Hector Elizondo and Joaquim De Almeida

During his career, he has directed numerous videos and second units and has served as production manager for such feature films as *What Dreams May Come, Tombstone, Total Recall, Rambo III,* and *Friday the 13th.* Additionally, he was production executive on such features as *Die Hard with a Vengeance* directed by John McTierman and *Scarlet Letter* directed by Roland Joffee.

Terry produced *Shadow Conspiracy* for Cinergi Pictures, Eugenio Zanetti's *Quantum Project,* and the *Daylight* miniature unit for Rafaella Productions.

Terry's experience in filmmaking is international in scope. He has filmed in Canada, Mexico, Israel, Thailand, Italy, Costa Rica, and Puerto Rico.

Terry and Barnet at the Washington Oaks location

Beverly Camhe Producer

Beverly Camhe was a longtime supporter of making *The Celestine Prophecy* into a movie. Because of her personal interests and her career in moviemaking, she read the book and dreamed of producing it; but there was a mad frenzy going on in Hollywood in the early 1990s to get the rights to the book, so Beverly waited for some synchronistic magic to occur.

Beverly's concern was that the movie would not be done faithfully to the book's purpose, so when she learned that the Redfields had also had reservations and not chosen a producer, she arranged a meeting with James's publishing attorney, John Diamond, in Los Angeles to discuss her passion for the project. An unusual stormy day had delayed Diamond's arrival at a Studio City office. When he entered the high-rise suite, he encountered Beverly sitting in front of a picture window where a vivid rainbow had formed a halo above her head. Before he could react, his cell phone rang, and it was James calling to say, "I have a feeling the right person is going to come into our lives today." John Diamond stared at the rainbow-adorned Beverly and replied, "I think she already has."

The next day Beverly met the Redfields for the first time in Sedona, where they were speaking, and she stayed with the project for seven years until it went in production.

"James and I agreed that a prologue was essential to cosmically link the destiny of the film characters and to establish that they were all together in an ancient past life. This structure would also allow the use of dreams and intuitions in the plot development."

Beverly Camhe has been in the entertainment industry for 25 years. She began her career as a literary manager working with playwrights, composers, and lyricists. Then she managed The Urban Art Corps, the African American theater company that produced the Broadway hit *Your Arm's Too Short to Box with God*. She went on to develop dramatic programming for David Frost while he was doing his groundbreaking television journalism, such as *The Nixon Interviews*. Beverly then worked with Tomorrow Medcom Entertainment, the company that spawned reality television. They produced the Emmy Award-winning series *The Body Human* and the first reality series in medicine—*Lifeline*—for NBC.

As VP of Martin Poll Productions, she developed the script for the Sylvester Stallone feature *Nighthawks*. Beverly then became Senior VP, Movies and Miniseries, for Lorimar Television during the company's heyday of *Dallas*, *Knots Landing*, and their many award-winning miniseries, including *Helter Skelter*. She also served as a Senior VP of Development for David Susskind Productions at MGM-UA. Beverly then joined Gabriel Katzka in a production company that produced *The Falcon and the Snowman*.

As Beverly Camhe Productions, she produced *The Believers* for Orion Pictures, directed by John Schlesinger and starring Martin Sheen; *The Package,* starring Gene Hackman and Tommy Lee Jones; and *Junior,* with Arnold Schwarzenegger and Danny De Vito. Her most recent efforts are *Car Talk,* an animated series based on the PBS radio show, and *Pepe and Stefano,* a film based on her own script.

Michael Givens
Director of Photography

*F*or more than 15 years Michael Givens has been the very successful director of photography (DP) for brand-name television commercials shot all over the world. In one two-year period, he was behind the motion picture camera 650 days. His long-form experiences include 35 feature films in the camera departments of such noted directors as Ridley Scott, Steven Friers, Philip Borsos, and Peter Smilie.

Michael caught the wave of synchronicity that led him to filming of *The Celestine Prophecy* by inquiring of professional friend Darryl Beckerleg, "What are you working on?" A call to Terry Collis led to an invitation to submit a sample DVD and subsequently to meet the producers, author James Redfield, and director Armand Mastroianni, who were giving the final approval for the Ocala location that was the key to filming in Florida. They were convening at the Ocala Hilton, so Michael drove from his home in Beaufort, South Carolina, to discuss the look of the planned film. Michael assured James Redfield that "what you can think, you can do" in the technology of today's filmmaking. Michael also had ideas for color correction and a method to get a bonus out of raw film footage.

Of Armand, Michael says, "He makes me want to find his vision. He is the kindest, gentlest kind of director. There is lots of hugging on this set."

Michael trusts the location itself to give him an intuitive recognition for camera placement and lighting. This deep sensitivity to intention and synchronicity is what brought him into the filming of *The Celestine Prophecy*.

Michael's most recent project is *Father of His Country*, a biopic of George Washington, for Piedmont Pictures.

Matthew Settle as John Woodson

"Armand is wonderful in that he doesn't give you anything negative. He always comes back with a laugh or makes a joke. Will you try it this way for me? He also listens, which is a great push and pull, which is what collaboration should be.

"I've been a fan of Thomas Kretschmann for years. I worked with him on *U-571* where he sort of took me under his wing. It's great to bring our natural friendship to the roles of John and Wil.

"Sarah Wayne Callies is beautiful. The camera loves her. We both can be intellectually feisty, like two cats on a clothesline, so our personalities turned out to be perfect casting for the tension between John and Marjorie.

"Joaquim De Almeida is great for Father Sanchez because he gets to say important lines that could be so preachy coming from a less veteran actor. Joaquim is totally at ease with himself, and thus he doesn't feel the need to sell anything."

Matthew Settle had come to a point that Solomon described in the Bible as "the gain of knowledge that brings a mind to sadness." Only weeks before he discussed *The Celestine Prophecy* lead role with James Redfield and Barnet Bain, Matthew had already begun to seek a restoration of faith and purpose in his personal life. Something was happening—a strange linking of events and people to effect the practice of a new idea that would foster self-awareness and a gratefulness, a thanksgiving, for all relationships and experiences that had culminated in his present moments. This personal journey was openly revealed to James and Barnet in their first meeting.

When Matthew first read the film script, he identified with John's spiritual journey, but he wondered if he could find the voice within himself to be faithful to the character. The dialog had to be spoken naturally, with no trace of self-conscious affectation, because the content was spiritually significant. In no way could the dialog drift into preachiness. It must be organic and authentic. Since acting, for Matthew, is an opportunity to learn and explore, the spiritual journey of John in *The Celestine Prophecy* proved to be synchronized to Matthew's own path to find a balance between love, power, and intelligence. In the film, John surrenders his past as a prologue to growth, and he finds no laments to prevent an acceptance that brings wholeness and satisfaction in all relationships. This, too, was the goal of the actor, and the evidence can be seen on screen as a faithful performance.

Matthew Settle starred as the young Warren Beatty in the ABC Premiere Event *The Mystery of Natalie Wood*, directed by Peter Bogdanovich. Starring opposite Ashley Judd in Director Callie Khouri's *Divine Secrets of the Ya-Ya Sisterhood*, Matthew played her true love, an ill-fated soldier who is lost to

war. With upcoming films including *Rancid* and *Until the Night*, his feature credits include *U-571*, *Attraction*, and *I Still Know What You Did Last Summer* with Jennifer Love Hewitt. On television he portrayed the legendary Captain Ronald Speirs in Steven Spielberg and Tom Hanks's award-winning HBO production of *Band of Brothers* and starred opposite Ann-Margret in *A Place Called Home* for Hallmark.

Matthew can be seen in 2005 as Jacob Wheeler in the TV miniseries *Into the West*, a nineteenth-century adventure of two families—white and Indian. He was also the host of *Decisive Battles*, a TV documentary series.

Sarah Wayne Callies as Marjorie

"Marjorie is so much fun to play because she thinks that she is centered and focused, but at the same time, she can totally freak out. On the page, Marjorie can be very sharp and even bitter. Armand gave me a great direction when he said to me as Marjorie, 'You're not mean, you're just protecting yourself.'

"This movie has an incredible ensemble that believes in the story we're telling, its merits and its values. James's presence on the set is critical. I can't imagine that we could have done it without him.

"I read *The Celestine Prophecy* when I was in high school, and it has resonated with me in a profound way ever since. Imagine how I feel that this film is the start of my movie career. And as long as this film hits the audience in their hearts, I'm happy."

Sarah Wayne Callies starred as Jane Porter in the series *Tarzan* and was cast as the lead in ABC's *The Service*. She makes her feature film debut in *The Celestine Prophecy*.

Raised in Hawaii, the daughter of university professors, Callies grew up in Honolulu. After earning undergraduate degrees in Drama and Feminist Studies and a Senior Fellowship in Indigenous Theology from Dartmouth College, she attended the National Theater Conservatory in Denver, where she earned her masters of fine arts degree.

Her first professional role was in Oliver Platt's *Queens Supreme*, which was followed by appearances on *Law and Order: SVU* and the *L.A. Dragnet* television series.

Chosen as one of the new faces of L'Oréal, she is featured in advertising campaigns for the international cosmetics company.

Joaquim De Almeida as Father Sanchez

"Father Sanchez is a compilation of a lot of characters from the book. In the movie, I am the conductor of *The Celestine Prophecy*, especially with regard to John. Father Sanchez thinks that the *Prophecy* helps every religion come alive. The Insights are universal. He tries to explain the importance of the scrolls to his former mentor, Cardinal Sebastian, but the opposition of General Rodriguez is too strong to prevent the destruction of the scrolls and the Celestine ruins and to protect the lives of the seekers of the Ninth Insight.

"I have played six priests in several languages and a lot of bad guys in American films. It's nice to play a good guy for a change. I hope audiences experience what James wrote in his book—that we can live in the world in a different way through love and being aware of nature. We need to live in this world in an insightful way."

Joaquim De Almeida has appeared in over 40 feature films in Europe and the United States and worked with some of the world's most distinguished actors and directors. De Almeida made his American film debut in *The Soldier* and went on to appear opposite Richard Gere and Michael Caine in *Honorary Consul*. He starred with Marisa Tomei and Robert Downey, Jr., in Norman Jewison's *Only You*, and opposite Harrison Ford in Philip Noyce's *Clear and Present Danger*. He most recently starred with Daryl Hannah and Denise Richards in Luna's *Yo Puta* (The Whore), the latest in a string of European film productions in which he stars.

Other notable films include Robert Rodriguez's *Desperado* with Antonio Banderas and Salma Hayek, and John Moore's *Behind Enemy Lines* opposite Gene Hackman. Among his many television credits are recurring roles on NBC's hit series *The West Wing* and Fox's award-winning *24* with Keifer Sutherland. De Almeida's American stage work includes the Kennedy Center production of *The Count of Monte Cristo*, directed by Peter Sellars, as well as productions by the Lee Strasberg Institute and the New York Shakespeare Festival. De Almeida divides his time between homes in his native Portugal and Los Angeles. He can be seen in the 2005 films *Thanks to Gravity* and *Posdata*.

Annabeth Gish as Julia

"Julia is very peaceful and perceptive, very intuitive. I think that she's the love piece in this movie in terms of Mother Earth. She is very serene in nature and in her relationships with the other characters. I think that she embodies the Celestine Insights. Julia is a teacher to John and a partner to Wil. Then there is a whole story line about how Julia is childless and how she has wanted a child for a long time and how she is rewarded in a deep and moving way with a beautiful child.

"I read *The Celestine Prophecy* when it came out, and I resonated with the Insights because of my interest in metaphysical studies. Then a remarkable synchronistic event propelled me into this film. I was on a plane from Jacksonville to Los Angeles when my seat mate confided to me that he had just met the woman of his dreams, and her name was Julia. I wrote in my day book that something magical was about to happen. I don't know why. Then when I landed in Los Angeles, urgent messages reached me. I was wanted for the role of "Julia" in *The Celestine Prophecy*, and the casting interview was back in Jacksonville!

"I've thought a lot about Salle Redfield as a role model for Julia because she sends energy to all of us in such a quiet, supportive way. I think of Julia as a soldier of the scrolls and as someone, like Salle and James, who gives love enough to rearrange the synapses of the heart. And that's really my hope for the audiences who see this movie—that we move the inner heart of their consciousness."

Annabeth Gish is one of the most consistently impressive and diverse young actresses working today. Gish, who plays President Bartlett's older daughter on NBC's Emmy-winning drama *The West Wing*, will next be seen on the big screen in the independent feature film *Knots*.

Gish first gained the attention of critics and moviegoers at the age of 13 when, according to film critic Roger Ebert, she delivered a performance of "stunning power" in the feature film *Desert Bloom*. She went on to star in the acclaimed *Mystic Pizza* with Julia Roberts before taking a four-year break from her career to attend Duke University, graduating cum laude with a degree in English.

Gish previously portrayed FBI Special Agent Monica Reyes on Fox's critically acclaimed series *The X-Files*. She will next be seen on television starring opposite Tom Berenger and Cybill Shepherd in the miniseries *Detective*, a psychological thriller for the USA Network, and in Stephen King's TV miniseries *Desperation* with Tom Skerritt, Steven Weber, and Ron Perlman.

Thomas Kretschmann as Wil

"When I look at James, he seems to me a cowboy version of a Buddha. He's balanced and smiley, and he doesn't take things for granted. I try to observe him and pick up things from him because, at least for me, James is the role model for Wil.

"Matthew wears me out sometimes, but he has a beautiful heart, and he fights so much for his part because the role is a journey for him as a human being. That is true for me as well. I have children so I need to calm down in everyday life and remind myself of my blessings. Working in this film is a lesson about being balanced."

Thomas Kretschmann is best known as the compassionate Nazi officer who spares the life of Adrien Brody's Wladyslaw Szpilman in Roman Polanski's Academy Award-winning *The Pianist*.

Born in East Germany in a region plagued with multinational politics, Kretschmann ultimately escaped to West Berlin, where he chose acting over his original goal of becoming an Olympic swimmer. Kretschmann made his 1991 acting debut in the television production of *Der Mitwisser* in a role for which he earned Germany's prestigious Max Ophuls Prize. Among his film credits are *U-571* and *Blade II*.

Thomas has remained busy with *Head in the Clouds* opposite Charlize Theron; *Butterfly, A Grimm Love Story*, where he portrays a cannibal killer; and *King Kong*, an epic remake of the classic, co-starring Naomi Watts, Jack Black, and Adrien Brody, and directed by Peter Jackson. In 2005, he also starred in the German film *Schneeland*, a very intense Nordic film about depression and parental abuse.

Hector Elizondo as Cardinal Sebastian

"This movie might help individuals to learn how to listen, to really listen, and really feel and find out what they're here to do instead of being isolated egos wrapped in a bag of skin trying to do a lot of shopping.

"Cardinal Sebastian is an inflexible force who feels threatened. He is not a villain. He has his own point of view, and he thinks that he is serving God by protecting the position of his church. And yet, there is a chance for this character to become truly introspective, and I think that he does by the end of the film.

"Armand knows how to coax. He knows how to find the right phrase. Then while the actor is practicing his craft, the director is actually supposed to disappear, and that's what Armand does. He's a working-class guy like I am. He's a person. He's a mensch.

"Humanity is still trying to solve deep and horrible problems from our reptilian past in the same stupid ways, so anything that points to an alternative to solving the human connection problem is a very important effort. That's why I think *The Celestine Prophecy* is an important film."

Hector Elizondo is a four-time Emmy nominee who received the prestigious award in 1997 as Outstanding Supporting Actor in a Drama Series for his portrayal of Dr. Phillip Watters on CBS's *Chicago Hope*.

One of those rare actors who continues to move back and forth freely between starring roles on Broadway, television, and feature films, he was nominated for a Golden Globe Award for his memorable portrayal of a hotel manager in the mega feature hit *Pretty Woman*.

Elizondo has appeared in more than 80 films, including *Raising Helen*, *Princess Diaries I & II*, *Tortilla Soup*, *Runaway Bride*, *Beverly Hills Cop III*, *Getting Even with Dad*, and *Frankie and Johnny*. In addition to his big-screen success, Elizondo starred in the critically acclaimed Broadway revival of Arthur Miller's *The Price* alongside Eli Wallach at the Roundabout Theatre.

A native New Yorker, Elizondo first gained recognition on the New York stage for his portrayal of God in *Steambath*, a performance which earned him an Obie Award. High praise followed for his Broadway role in *The Great White Hope*, *Sly Fox*, and Neil Simon's *Prisoner of Second Avenue*, for which he received a Drama Desk Award nomination. Look for Hector in the lead role as Popo in the 2005 film *I Believe in America*.

Jürgen Prochnow
as Jensen

"Jensen is a great enigma. He is a gangster, but he is also a secret agent who opposes the nature of spirituality. This guy is totally against the beauty of people's minds and what they can create because he only believes in material power and control. He's pretty deadly.

"I like the prologue scenes that go back hundreds of years. The action shots were very, very good stuff. The birthmark on the nobleman who betrays the Celestine ruins worshipers is seen again in modern times on Jensen's arm. The character is consistent from one age to another, and he is very interesting to me, far more interesting than the usual villains in action movies. *The Celestine Prophecy* is something very unusual and something new."

Jürgen Prochnow has appeared in over 50 feature films and countless television productions in the United States and Europe.

A native of Germany born in Dusseldorf, he is best known for his unforgettable performance as the submarine commander in the gripping drama *Das Boot.* Prochnow appeared with Yun-Fat Chow and Mira Sorvino in Antoine Fuqua's *The Replacement Killers* and opposite Harrison Ford in Wolfgang Peterson's *Air Force One.* Among his many film credits are Anthony Minghella's *The English Patient,* David Lynch's *Dune,* John Carpenter's *In the Mouth of Madness,* as well as *A Dry White Season, Judge Dredd,* and *Beverly Hills Cop II.*

In 2005 Jürgen starred in the role of Arnold Schwarzenegger, with Mariel Hemingway as Maria Shriver, in the television film *See Arnold Run.*

Rachel Erickson as The Little Girl

Rachel Erickson did not attend the major casting call that might have made her the special child featured in *The Celestine Prophecy;* nevertheless, on the strength of her photograph submitted by a talent agent, Rachel was invited to the callback, where she got the job.

Rachel, however, had already proven her star power. After seeing the aftermath of 9/11 on television, Rachel went to her room and began singing *The Star-Spangled Banner* as a personal way of dealing with the crisis. Her mother, Francis, was amazed and called Tampa radio station WYUU-U92. Radio show host Mason Dixon asked to hear Rachel sing and put her passionate rendering of the national anthem out over the air. Rachel was seven years old. The audience response was fantastic. Rachel was asked to perform the national anthem to open the Lee Greenwood and Charlie Daniels concert; and then in 2002, she sang for U.S. Central Command's Commander-in-Chief General Tommy Franks and 2,000 guests at the anniversary observance of Operation Enduring Freedom. She got a standing ovation wherever she sang, and General Franks was quoted as saying that he had heard the national anthem sung two or three thousand times during his military career, all kinds of versions of it, "But I never heard anyone do a better job than Rachel."

Rachel appears in several major scenes of the film. It is her first acting role. She has no lines, but her sweet face virtually sings.

Jim Schoppe
Production Designer

Jim works with Barnet on the bus explosion.

James L. "Jim" Schoppe began his career in films as an art director and production designer in 1972. He had a great release year in 1979 as art director for *The Rose*, Bette Midler's starring debut, and *Being There*, the classic with Peter Sellers and Shirley MacLaine. In 1983, he received an Academy Award nomination with two others for art direction of George Lucas's *Star Wars: Return of the Jedi*. Jim was very busy in the '80s and '90s with films such as *Revenge of the Nerds*, *Volunteers* with Tom Hanks and John Candy, *Over the Top* with an arm-wrestling Sylvester Stallone, and *The Color of Night* with Bruce Willis. By the mid '80s, Jim was a full-fledged production designer, playing a significant role in the look of the films on which he worked.

Terry Collis, as production manager, worked with Jim, the production designer, on *The Color of Night*. Jim had read *The Celestine Prophecy* with his wife in the mid-1990s; and, as a result, he had an immediate interest in the movie project. The design challenge was to get the proper look that not only complemented the novel but also showed the energy fields that on screen would give the audience a unique psychic perspective.

In discussions with James Redfield especially, spiritual inspiration and film technology needed to meet in concepts that could be translated to storyboards and later to film. Thus Jim's design research included the Peruvian rainforest, Spanish colonial architecture, Mayan ruins, as well as the look of auras and energy fields. A great deal of effort was put into the planning of visual effects, and James Redfield got high marks for an amazing crash course in graduate level moviemaking.

"This film was one of the best professional experiences that I have had in 20 years. The absence of ego and conflict, plus the fact that it was a worthwhile project with quality values, made it very special to me. I am still amazed at the reach of the original novel and the extent of its influence.

"Hats off, too, to the construction crew and the painters who met every production deadline. And all of us have to give thanks, finally, for the perfect weather. We did not lose a single day to rain."

CELESTINE PROPHECY
THE MOVIE

Suzy Freeman
Costume Designer

For a shooting day that involves dressed extras as well as featured actors, Costume Designer Suzy Freeman—a pert, petite, brunette, 15-year professional trained in the Royal Academy of Dramatic Arts in London—begins her work more than two hours before sunrise. Suzy's work base is a 48-foot trailer lined with rows of costumes labeled for each cast member. A ladder is needed to access the top double racks. Between the racks of clothing, there are work stations for sewing machines; but in good weather, the work goes outside under a canopy where a costume supervisor, three set costumers, and a seamstress or two work to organize the garments and accessories for the day's scenes.

The team is continually doing fittings. Suzy has an office in the trailer with a washer and dryer, but the action of costuming must follow the cast to their own personal dressing trailers, or to a large tent provided for the extras, and then to the set itself. It is not unusual to dress 35 people for an 8:30 A.M. set call.

Before the base camp trailer was filled with clothing and accessories, of course the costumes had to be conceived, purchased, leased, or manufactured. Much of the period costuming for the conquistadors in the prologue scenes was leased, but most of the clothing for the principal actors was custom fitted and manufactured by Suzy and her crew specifically for *The Celestine Prophecy*.

Suzy is very aware of choosing a color palette in her costume

Suzy fits Thomas Kretschmann in the wardrobe trailer.

design that not only compliments and identifies an actor, but also serves the overall look of the film as planned by the art department. The character John, for example, is seen wearing browns and is thus differentiated in a scene with Wil, whose color palette tends toward greens. Suzy also must be aware of scenes shot in front of the blue screen, where special effects will be added later. No actor in those scenes can be wearing blue.

Suzy read *The Celestine Prophecy* cover to cover on a flight from Florida to London in the mid-1990s when people on both sides of the Atlantic were discussing James Redfield's remarkable book.

"It was during a life- and career-changing period in my life," she recalls. "*The Celestine Prophecy* was the first opportunity for me to redefine spirituality after a strict Catholic education. I never imagined that I would become the costume designer for the making of the book into a movie."

When the camera comes in for close-ups, the neck and sleeve trim on a garment appears on the theater screen as wide as a refrigerator. At that size, there is no way to fake authenticity. Many of the fabrics worn by featured players and extras were imported from Peru and then cut, sewn, manufactured, and fitted for the film. In one stroke of synchronicity, as costumes were being assembled in the St. Augustine production building, Location Manager Rick Ambrose learned that gallery owner and local artist Deanne Kellogg was going to Lima, Peru, on a long-planned vacation. Suzy reacted fast and gave Deanne funds to purchase hand-woven goods in the rural mountain markets above Lima. What she brought back was a treasure of fabric handicrafts that were incorporated into many costumes. Their color and weave added undeniable Peruvian authenticity; and what's more, the goods that she returned to St. Augustine were blessed by Peruvian village elders for use in the film.

Although *The Celestine Prophecy* was Suzy's first feature as costume designer, her second—*Things That Hang from Trees*—began shooting in spring of 2005, soon after she worked as a costume supervisor on *All the King's Men* with Sean Penn and Jude Law. Suzy has also dressed Ben Kingsley, John Travolta, Dustin Hoffman, Bill Murray, Willem Dafoe, and many other star talents on sets across Europe and America.

Suzy fits an extra with authentic Peruvian accents as her seamstresses work in the background.

The Shared Vision

First assistant director Carl Ludwig, Terry Collis, Armand Mastroianni, James Redfield, Barnet Bain, and Jim Schoppe review a major scene setup.

*Y*outhful, buoyant, charming, and affectionate. Those are the words that come to mind when you encounter Armand Mastroianni. His intensity is that of a father or a brother giving advice. He demonstrates the director's essential quality—patience—when he counsels his actors into giving their best performance.

If anyone shouts or barks, "Quiet please, rolling, sound, action, cut, and check the gate," it is first assistant director Carl Ludwig. Carl is tall (made taller by the Western-style straw hat that he wore during the shoot) and commanding in a good-humored Austrian-accented way. Carl and the serious-faced second assistant director Jack Steinberg are the satellites of Armand's directions. Where they are loud, Armand is quiet and reflective, more intimate with the actors and crew in discussing the needs of a scene.

In filming, Armand is usually seen standing in front of the "A" and "B" cameras monitor watching the scene intently. He has already done his primary job with the actors, his DP (director of photography), and his assistants; so the picture on the monitor shows him what he needs to see, what the theater audience will see, and more importantly, what they will feel.

But behind the techniques of filmmaking, and even the traits of personality, is a higher calling for a wisdom that serves the nature of true collaboration. The content of personal spiritual growth and the issues of consciousness that *The Celestine Prophecy* explores must be demonstrated in the actual making of the movie. The process itself, from script writing to the final edit in post-production, must celebrate the reality of lives lived in synchronistic harmony. The spiritual awakening that the millions of people worldwide responded to in James Redfield's novel must also be felt in the movie as the filmmakers implement their most inspired dreams. This is the personal opportunity available to both filmmakers and the audience, but the experiencers are not separated in time. They rather share a common visionary experience that unites all individual minds in a relationship without boundaries, without restrictions.

Armand is a director of movement. He puts his actors in movement to heighten the drama and to parallel the psycho-spiritual movement that is occurring internally. The style of this movement is not imposed on the characters but is rather encouraged as an expressive freedom. When Armand approaches an actor with suggestions for additional takes of a scene, his directions appear from a distance to be gentle whisperings. Behind the camera, from a position of the tall director's chairs lined up behind the monitors, one can wonder if director Armand Mastroianni ever shouts. And yet, when you see him work, there is an obvious energy that can only be described as passion, but the passion is confidently ebullient, not strident or invading. Armand is a soul who nurtures, and thus his attributes are a synchronistic match for *The Celestine Prophecy* story and the insights that James Redfield hoped to share through his literature, and now through the movie.

Salle and James listen to Armand's concept for the next scene.

When Sarah Wayne Callies (as Marjorie) tells Matthew Settle (as John) what she wants in a relationship, she defines for all of us the spiritual nature of behavior, a behavior that is neither insecure nor controlling—behavior between married couples, dating couples, parents and children, friends and strangers that is not a power struggle. It is James Redfield's Eighth Insight. "Instead of *taking* energy from each other, you give it. All the time. No matter what."

Energy, in the fulfillment of *The Celestine Prophecy*, becomes another name for love. In the new reality of how coincidences led us to transforming insights, we are free to express the true nature of our beingness. In *The Celestine Prophecy*, this happy enlightenment is seen as the direction of human evolution.

The movement of the film is a movement of the heart that reveals the underlying truth of relationship. The character John Woodson, the narrator, makes that journey for us, and with us; and he discovers, as we must, the Insights one by one until he has not only the understanding, but also the experience, of the Ninth Insight. The journey in the film is more than metaphysical; it is actual and, for those who will take it, transforming.

In the same way that a viewer is required to suspend personal ambitions and frustrations in order to take

The Celestine Prophecy spiritual journey, so, too, are the filmmakers. For the journey is not about the conditioned self. That concept of self is earthbound. That image of self cannot soar to its potential. That self is limited. The true Self, the Self connected to infinite wisdom, is unlimited. Living as the true Self is a moving meditation where even apparent conflicts are synchronistic touchstones for increased wisdom and beauty. The promise of *The Celestine Prophecy* is known in American Indian metaphysics as "the walk in beauty." *The Celestine Prophecy* provides a way, a realization, that each of us has the opportunity to walk in beauty.

Director Armand Mastroianni and script authors and co-producers James Redfield and Barnet Bain held in mutual trust, faith, and confidence the vision that *The Celestine Prophecy*, the movie, became. Their synchronicity was paramount in the development of the project. From their triumvir emanated the energy that permeated every decision. They held the context, the bubble of visionary light, that inspired and protected the integrity of the message that so many individuals had responded to worldwide. The responsibility for adapting the book into the movie might have been an awesome task had they not held the faith of the Insights themselves. They knew that life lived is not linear, that it flows through great, interconnected dimensions that are available to us for complete success in every heart-conscious endeavor. This consciousness allows for fearlessness in the great adventure of relationships. It also allows for spiritually conscious filmmaking.

Armand blocks a shot with actor Jürgen Prochnow and director of photography Michael Givens.

The Adventure Begins

John discovers a coincidence in the mail.

A young man in the prime of his expectations is utterly disappointed by life. He feels wasted as a high school teacher, and his most recent romantic relationship has just failed. Depressed and seemingly out of viable options, John Woodson is poised to begin the adventure of self-discovery. All that he has to do is follow his intuitions and recognize the synchronicities that are about to present themselves.

First, there is an invitation to have supper with a friend on a coincidental airport layover. Charlene has been feeling that she should tell John about a priest she met in Peru and about the discovery of an ancient prophecy that was being studied at a remote jungle lodge named Viciente. Charlene even has the audacity to tell John that he should go to Peru.

Back at his cabin on a lake, John discovers a travel brochure on Peru in his stack of mail; and when he calls, mostly out of curiosity, he is offered an unbelievable deal if he will fill the seat of a cancellation and fly to Peru the next day. Caught up in the wave of intention, John is swept up in a movement that will radically change his awareness of what it means to be alive. And from this moment on, all his dreams, all his actions, and all his relationships will contribute to a wonderful series of Insights that are *The Celestine Prophecy*.

Charlene tells John about the Prophecy.

Robyn Cohen in the role of Charlene

In a chain of coincidences, John meets Professor Dobson (John Aylward), who also knows about the Prophecy.

Father José (Castulo Guerra) waits for the Prophecy seekers at his church in Lima.

The Prophecy says when we find the true connection with the energy of God . . . it's like a glimpse into the future. One day we'll all see that way and live in *that* world.

Washington Oaks

To replicate the tropical jungle of Peru, the producers of *The Celestine Prophecy* chose Washington Oaks State Gardens, a lush coastal landscape where ancient live oaks, hickories, and magnolias border the tidal marshes of the Mantazar River south of St. Augustine. A hill at the top of the rose garden formed by oyster shells attests to the generations of Native Americans who gathered shellfish and hunted in the area.

The 410-acre Washington Oaks site was part of the Belle Vista Plantation that the Spanish Floridian family of General Joseph Hernandez held for over a hundred years. In 1936, it was purchased by the family of Owen Young, then chairman of General Electric. In 1964, Mrs. Young donated the estate to the state so that it could be preserved as a botanical wonder.

Although the Gardens and its structures were used for a full week of filming, great care was exercised to respect the natural environment. Everyone who came to the location was both amazed and entranced by its beauty and pristine atmosphere. Deep into its network of dirt roads, one could easily believe that this jungle was Peru.

During a principal night shot, the dark was eerie with the twisted shapes of ancient live oaks rising like fingers beyond the lights. Cabbage palms spread their fans between the tree trunks, and "Burly" Bob Welch, the greens man, beat the scrub path into the forest so that the actors would not encounter snakes.

Away from the actual set was the Washington Oaks base camp, a small village on wheels that included the hair and make-up trailer, the wardrobe semi, cast trailers, producer-director trailers, the catering kitchen trailer serving main meals, and Reva Grantham's Craft Service kitchen serving snacks, beverages, and keep-'em-going soups and sandwiches. And lest we forget, the all-important eight-room honey wagon (crew bathrooms).

At base camp, a large tent with tables and chairs and a buffet table with beverages, salads, and condiments served as the dining area. The catering kitchen trailer served breakfast, lunch, and supper (when necessary).

On a working Saturday, the call sheet noted that the project lunch was scheduled for 5 P.M. Everyone looked forward to the lunch breaks that were always dependent on the completion of the shots on set. Chef Jeff Gardner (Shooting Star Catering) did not disappoint the hungry horde whenever it descended on him, and somehow he kept hot and ready a menu of three entrees—beef, chicken, and fish—plus enough variety in vegetables and side dishes to accommodate all diets.

On another road in Washington Oaks, the equipment trailers were parked. This was another center of activity with technical crew members working out of a ten-ton grip trailer, a ten-ton

electric trailer, a ten-ton camera trailer, a props semi, a special effects (SFX) semi, a five-ton set decoration trailer, a rigging ten-ton, plus a water truck, a fueler, stakebeds, and a picture car carrier. All of these warehouses-on-wheels had to be moved whenever the location changed.

At the production offices in St. Augustine, Bobbie Collis, the production coordinator, performed daily miracles to meet the needs of the entire company. Bobbie and her staff leased the locations, coordinated all travel and accommodations, and performed all the administration functions of jobs that always carried a short, if not immediate, deadline. That all this controlled chaos was done with great efficiency, warmth, and good humor seemed miraculous. Bobbie's favorite previous film jobs were *Thelma and Louise* and *Tombstone*. The two floors of the production office had desks and working space for more than 20 people and included space for the art department, editing, and wardrobe.

When Feng Shui Master Katherine Lewis was asked by James Redfield to organize the harmony of the office space, to her amazement, Katherine discovered that Bobbie had already placed producer, writer, director, and support staff in a perfect Feng Shui relationship.

In another example of synchronicity, the building that was leased to be the production offices was formerly a Barnett Bank building, only one letter removed from Barnet Bain, the film's producer and co-scriptwriter.

On that long Saturday, production designer Jim Schoppe was in Ocala at a quarry where the construction crew was building the Celestine ruins. Shooting at the ruins set was scheduled to begin in two weeks. The set had to be ready by then, no matter what. Jim's son Palmer, art department assistant, remained on the Washington Oaks set should problems develop there.

Storyboard artist James Mitchell, a visual effects consultant, and James Redfield worked at the production offices all morning on the final look of the scenes to be shot at the ruins set. Storyboarding and key decision-making were an ongoing daily event. Focus, concentration, and creative energies had to be maintained by everyone involved over an extended period of time. The joke around the set was that you could sleep in June, after the movie had wrapped.

On the Road to Viciente

Wil and John stop at a primitive gas station en route to Viciente.

Wil and John discuss the Prophecy at their campsite.

With Washington Oaks as a background, John and his guide to Viciente, Wil, take the road less traveled after an escape from enemies of the Prophecy in Lima. Wil reveals that he was with Father José when he found the ancient scrolls; and he describes Julia, the translator, and Father Sanchez, the philosopher, as primary seekers of the missing Ninth Insight. Wil tells a skeptical John that perhaps he has a role to play in the revelation of the Ninth Insight, but he will not tell John the content of the eight discovered scrolls.

"I could describe these insights to you right now, John, and you would hear the words . . . but you have to do *more* than that. You have to *experience* them yourself. *The Prophecy has to happen to you.*"

Costa Rica

The Land Cruiser comes across a man and
his pack mule on a narrow mountain road.

The red helicopter with Westcam tech Robert "Dan" Kelly and Westcam operator David Norris

To obtain the establishing shots and the aerial footage of a speeding Land Rover in a mountainous land-scape, a Second Unit crew of 17, plus director Armand Mastroianni, producers James and Salle Redfield, Barnet Bain, and Terry Collis, visual effects supervisors John Nugent and Nick Brooks, and production managers Darryl Beckerleg and Bobbie Collis traveled to the Monteverde Cloud Forest.

Monteverde, Costa Rica, is an ecotourist destination because it is one of the most outstanding wildlife refuges in the New World Tropics and, at 4,500 feet, the home of 100 species of mammals and 400 species of birds. This secluded and unspoiled rainforest environment is about 120 miles from the airport in San José, and a vehicular trip of three to four hours to Monteverde ends after 25 miles of jungle dirt roads.

The filming in August of 2004 took more than a week due to conditions of rain and fog. The film party stayed at the Cloud Forest Lodge, where manager Wilberth Parajeles proved so helpful and knowledgeable that he took on the role of location manager. The double for Matthew Settle was Robert Pate. Visual effects artists John and Nick shot plates of the rainforest canopy, detailed plant life, and mountain vistas for use in enhancing Insight sequences in the film. Barnet was onboard the swooping helicopter during filming to provide the air to ground coordination while Armand and the camera crew trekked the wet jungle for inspiring location shots.

Movie audiences might wonder how many of the 100 species of mammals the crew encountered. And how many spiders and snakes? Still, by all reports, Nature in its pristine state is wonderful.

Barnet and Armand take a humorous break during a fog delay.

At Viciente Lodge

Viciente Lodge's entryway at night

Miguel (Obba Babatunde), the host at Viciente

The Viciente Lodge, described in the book as an old nineteenth-century estate which formerly belonged to the Spanish Catholic Church, is a lush tropical place where searchers of the Celestine Insights gather and where scientists research the nature of pure energy "that is malleable to human intention and expectation in a way that defies our old mechanistic model of the universe."

In James Redfield's book, the Viciente Lodge is a focal point for the exploration of complex ideas that *The Celestine Prophecy* made so brilliantly accessible. Since so many key scenes of the movie occur at the Viciente Lodge, and because the millions of readers of *The Celestine Prophecy* have mental pictures of this unique place, the character of this location had to be outstanding.

Location manager Rick Ambrose found the palatial home of Fred and Lilly Vaill at Vaill Point and led James and Salle, Armand, Barnet, and Terry, the film's producers, to the site one hour before they were scheduled to leave the city. The isolated grounds, located on the Intracoastal Waterway, had verdant lawns and rich, colorful landscaping, surrounded by a woods of ancient live oaks and cabbage palms that matched the Washington Oaks Gardens where the environs of Peru would first be established. The sprawling 5,200-square-foot Spanish house with its courtyards was classic. Later, the filmmakers would learn that the house was named La Villa Bien Venidos, the House of Welcome.

Built in 1926 by Fred Vaill's father, the house was designed with the expectation that King Alphonso of Spain would one day visit St. Augustine and be a guest there. Fred Sr. had been knighted by the Spanish king in 1924 when he was among nine delegates from St. Augustine who accompanied the original coffin of Florida's first Royal Governor Pedro Menéndez de Avilés for re-interment in Spain. The rise of the Franco regime prevented King

John and Marjorie chat unsuccessfully.

Alphonso's state visit, but the great Spanish-styled home that once included 73 acres stood ready. Fred Jr. added three bedrooms and a large covered patio pool in 1972 to accommodate his four children. Some of the acreage has been developed, and some donated as a passive park to the state; but the Vaill family, who knew Henry Flagler himself during the early development of St. Augustine, still occupies the property.

The Vaill House as the Viciente Lodge was featured in three long days of day-and-night filming. An opening scene with principal characters Wil and Julia foreshadows the method for finding the Ninth Insight, the goal of the dedicated seekers. A scene that begins with Julia and John reinforces the play of synchronicity in the Viciente guests' coming together and the importance of dreams as a direction indicator.

An encounter between John and Marjorie, with Julia as the observer, reveals something amazing. Audiences, courtesy of Visual Effects, get to actually see the glowing energy fields that have heretofore been the sole province of psychics. In the scene, John's energy field is reaching out, drawing Marjorie's field into his. John is

The energies between the couple are revealed.

unaware of his aggressive exploitation of Marjorie's energy; but she feels it, hardens her face, steps back, and walks away. Julia is left to explain to John what has just occurred.

"It wasn't what you said," she tells John. "It was what you did. Your energy made her feel as though you wanted to control her. She felt dominated."

John, at this stage of experiencing the Insights, is still in denial about his unconscious behavior, and he is embarrassed. As audience, we have empathy for his mistakes, because we all know the place and have felt the rejection that unconscious, conditioned behavior generates in our lives. We walk emotionally with John in his quest to become a more sensitive, more successful human being. And just like in real life, we know that the road to self-awareness is often difficult.

The embodiment of John's difficulty, which is represented by the presence of fear, is the character Jensen, played by Jürgen Prochnow, the unforgettable face of the submarine commander in *Das Boot*, and the antagonist in such films as *Air Force One* opposite Harrison Ford. Like fear, Jensen can be both seductive and deadly.

Julia and Wil reunite at the lodge.

The impressive pool house at the Vaill estate becomes a meditation pool at Viciente Lodge. Wil and Julia speculate on John's spiritual growth, and Julia says, "I think he'll get there . . . unless, of course, he's too distracted."

One distraction for John is the beautiful Marjorie. After a dinner party, with the meditation pool as a backdrop, she stiffens at John's approach; but he behaves momentarily without self-interest, and she thus responds to his authenticity. John's energy, however, changes in the conversation, and Marjorie is immediately aware of it.

"It's funny how easy it is to lose yourself around certain people," she observes before she abruptly walks away. Marjorie's action is not the stuff of a romantic comedy; it is rather the product of an instructive interaction. John has to learn the lessons of the Insights so that they become his experience rather than a set of intellectual ideas.

Producer Beverly Camhe and marketing executive John Zimmerman make cameo appearances with Jürgen Prochnow in a Viciente dinner party scene.

Later in the Viciente gardens, Julia tries to help John understand what is occurring in his relationship with Marjorie. The Insight that she explains is not male-female, however. It is universal.

"People want to dominate and control because when they do, they get the other person's energy. It gives them a boost of power. But we don't have to build ourselves up that way by stealing energy. There's another source. Open yourself to the possibility that there's something more, right here in front of your eyes."

In a continuation of the film dialog, James Redfield, the author, stipulates the method for self-realization as Julia says, "Ask for it. Set an intention. Really expect it to happen. This isn't new. It's the real experience behind all religion, something that everyone senses, but few really discover. It's a process. You have to learn how to do it. Just be open to what you might see."

And in the scene, which is visually enhanced, John briefly gets it. He sees individual energy fields for a moment, but then he loses it. Yet, he has found the key. But how far can he go before fear intervenes?

John attempts to reconnect with Marjorie after the Viciente dinner party.

Jensen warns John about the dangers for those who seek the Prophecy.

In the next scene, Jensen appears at Viciente to thwart John's spiritual growth. Every spiritual seeker has his or her Jensens. They promise relief from doubts and routes to safety. They warn of dangers and offer false friendship. They are, in fact, experts in the theft of sacred energy. In *The Celestine Prophecy*, Jensen is the corrupting agent for the forces wedded to material and ideological power. Their greatest fear is that an enlightened world will not need them or their institutions of control and domination.

Later in the plot, Jensen prompts General Martez to attack Viciente and burn out the nest of Prophecy seekers.

Viciente is attacked and burned to the ground.

Energy between the Fingers

Julia instructs John on the presence of visible energy.

DP Michael Givens begins the camera setup for the "fingers" scene with characters John and Julia.

Armand directs the couple prior to filming.

Julia instructs John on the presence of visible energy.

Every reader of *The Celestine Prophecy* knows this scene and has probably tried to duplicate it with his or her own index fingers. In the scene, Julia (Annabeth Gish) helps John (Matthew Settle) to sense, and to actually see, the power of his own psychogenetic energy. John's brief experience opens the door to a series of Insights that forever alter his concept of the living reality.

With visual effects, the energy is now seen by the audience.

St. Augustine as Lima, Peru

To represent Lima, Peru, and its Spanish Renaissance architecture, the producers required buildings with massive iron gates, towers, domes, battlements, Spanish roof tiles, terra-cotta porticos, loggias, open galleries, corbels, sunny courts, cool fountain retreats, and decorations suggestive of a bygone historic era. They found it in St. Augustine, where, on a single square, stands one of the most impressive architectural complexes in late-nineteenth-century

American history. The quintessential Hotel Ponce de Leon (now Flagler College), the luxurious Alcazar Hotel (now the Lightner Museum), and Franklin Smith's companion Casa Monica Hotel all opened in 1888 to fulfill Henry Flagler's vision of the Florida east coast as an American Riviera. Flagler went on to build the Florida East Coast Railroad from Jacksonville to Key West and a string of 11 luxury resort hotels.

The Ponce de Leon was the first $100-a-day hotel in America, and the Alcazar contained the largest indoor swimming pool in the 1888 world. Casa Monica was restored to its former luxury hotel status in 1999 by Richard Kessler and was the headquarters hotel for cast and crew while they were in St. Augustine.

Flagler College

On April 13 the film crew occupied Flagler College, a unique architectural masterpiece that was built by Henry Flagler as the Hotel Ponce de Leon in 1888. Flagler, one of the original partners in Standard Oil, virtually invented tourism in Florida. His creation of a hotel to host the world's wealthiest clientele remains one of the best examples of Spanish-Moorish Renaissance architecture in the world. For *The Celestine Prophecy*, the restored Great Rotunda and lobby levels of the 2,000-student college provided the perfect location for the environs of the Peruvian Catholic Cardinal Sebastian, played by Emmy Award-winning actor Hector Elizondo.

The Great Rotunda rises over 80 feet in height amid a forest of carved wood and red marble columns. There are four arcades and overhanging galleries on three levels that give the feel of sixteenth-century cathedral magnificence. In this setting, Cardinal Sebastian and General Martez (Petrus Antonius) discuss the threat that the Celestine manuscript poses to their common interests. Both men fear the revolutionary ideas in the Insights. Cardinal Sebastian bids the general farewell on a broad staircase of marble and Mexican onyx that leads from the second gallery to the mosaic marble floor below.

In a critical dramatic scene filmed in a second-level alcove of the great dome, Cardinal Sebastian stands against the arguments of Father Sanchez (played by Joaquim De Almeida) that the ancient Celestine manuscripts do not work against Christianity or any other religion. Sanchez makes a plea on behalf of the Insights that James Redfield articulated so well in the book—the manuscript as a whole "doesn't negate, but clarifies the truth of the Church. The insights expand our spirituality," Sanchez says. "The Manuscript describes the inspiration that comes when we are truly loving others and evolving our lives forward."

Cardinal Sebastian (Hector Elizondo) discusses the problem of the Prophecy scrolls with General Martez (Petrus Antonius).

Flagler students gathered on the marble steps to their dining hall to view the filmmaking above their heads in the dome galleries. The stained glass windows above the east and west staircases are original Tiffany creations. The filming of *The Celestine Prophecy* may have been a one-day curiosity for the students who witnessed it, but the real benefit was to come the next school year. As part of the agreement to use Flagler College as a location, a very clever Brian Thompson, director of public information for the college, negotiated for James Redfield to return to campus as a writer-in-residence.

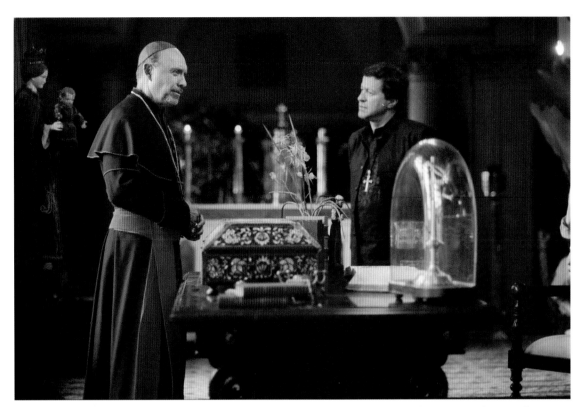

Father Sanchez (Joaquim De Almeida) makes a case to the cardinal for saving the scrolls.

Director Armand Mastroianni and author James Redfield discuss a scene with Hector Elizondo.

Set Decoration in the Historic Government House

Vera Mills, set decorator

Set decorator Vera Mills begins her job soon after the locations of the film are secured. Vera and her leadman, Norman Dulaney, tour the locations with production designer Jim Schoppe to discuss his vision of the look of the sets as they pertain to the film script. Vera had two advantages in dressing *The Celestine Prophecy* sets. First, she had read James Redfield's book when it first appeared in hardback; and second, she had worked with Jim on a major TV movie. Vera was also the art director for *Saved by the Light* with Eric Roberts.

After Jim and Vera are in agreement about the general look of the individual sets—all 30 of them that appear in *The Celestine Prophecy*—the individual locations are photographed for reference and planning. Vera then breaks down the script scene by scene and types up a master plan that details the items that she will need to dress each set. The items in the plan range from Persian carpets and period furniture to what will appear in a Catholic cardinal's office. Many of these decisions require detailed research and a decorator's sensitivity for color and composition. The extensive planning, however, is only one element of Vera's craft expertise. The real secret of her profession is knowing where to find the myriad thousands of items on the scene lists. Once the set decorating plan and budget are approved, Vera goes shopping.

During filming, leadman Norm directs the five-person crew and handles the logistics for three 24-foot trucks and a support warehouse. The handling of each item has a strict inventory control. Items secured from vendors are photographed in the development stage and

Cardinal Sebastian (Hector Elizondo) talks with General Martez (Petrus Antonius) about the Prophecy seekers at Viciente.

then rephotographed when they are secured. The vendor files are kept in 9 x 12 envelopes that contain contact information, rental agreements, and check requests from the production accounting department. A running inventory is kept of every item, but the miles traveled in securing and returning them are inconceivable.

Set decorators work early on location. Vera and her crew of five begin their workday at 5 A.M. On Tuesday, April 13, they dressed three interior sets within the historic Government House in St. Augustine and an exterior set half a block away at the Lightner Museum Building. Two of the big trucks and Vera's office van were required for the job. One room in the oldest section of Government House that dates from 1706 on a site occupied since 1596 was dressed for two separate scenes. Half the room became a general's military office and the other half a hotel room in Lima used by the character John. A change in camera positions was all that was required, a neat trick performed by experts in breaking down a script into its scene sets.

The next morning Vera waits for the film negative report from production manager Terry Collis that tells her that the set can be struck. Only then can her crew strike the set of production items and restore the location to its original condition if it was leased. Two truckloads and hours later, the items are returned to the warehouse for reuse or return and the trucks reloaded for the next day's set dress.

General Martez (Petrus Antonius) is threatened by Jensen (Jürgen Prochnow).

The set decorator's function is probably the most subject to change. On the set, she must respond immediately to the needs of the director and the production designer; and if, for any reason, a set must be reshot, Vera must remember the exact position of every item in view. Flexibility and endurance, mixed with artistic sensitivity and good humor, are the essential prerequisites.

Vera Mills has been a decorator on nearly 20 theatrical and television films. Additional credits include music videos and national television commercials as either art director or set decorator.

Government House served as the interior for General Martez's National Police headquarters; and in these rooms Cardinal Sebastian seeks control of the scrolls, and Jensen threatens the general so that he will cooperate in the destruction of the Prophecy and its seekers.

Director Armand Mastroianni directs Jürgen Prochnow on lighting the cigar.

Pioneers in the Spiritual Landscape

St. Augustine, aside from being a match for Spanish Colonial Peru's capital city Lima, also personifies a metaphorical connection to *The Celestine Prophecy*. St. Augustine stands as the beginning colony for the European habitation of North America because its 1565 settlement by Spain in La Florida predated the English arrival at Jamestown by 42 years and their landing of the *Mayflower* at Plymouth Rock by 55 years.

In the same way that St. Augustine was a new beginning, the Insights of *The Celestine Prophecy* promise a new beginning for the character John. He, too, has landed in a virgin country, but his new territory is the stuff of spiritual reality rather than terra firma. The seekers of the Celestine manuscript and its Nine Insights are colonists of a new idea; and the fate of human civilization, according to James Redfield in the novel, hangs on their understanding and dissemination of these truths.

The characters John, Wil, Julia, Marjorie, Sanchez, and Father José form

Location Fidelity

In the scene where armed men in police uniforms search for John in the Government House location, one of the three policemen extras was Jonzalo Delgado, a native of Lima, Peru, who has worked in the United States for eight years. How well did St. Augustine stand in for Lima in his opinion?

"Very well. The vegetation is the same, and so is the colonial architecture. No mountains, of course, but St. Augustine is cleaner and has a lot less air pollution."

the core group of characters of this bold attempt to redefine the direction of Beingness in a hostile environment. In many ways, they resemble the Spanish explorers who searched for new worlds and were willing to risk their lives in the attempt. The difference between *The Celestine Prophecy* explorers and the nation builders, however, is that the spiritual seekers carry no flag and seek no domination or control over lands or peoples. The seekers in *The Celestine Prophecy* are not in search of gold; they are rather focused on a goal. Their goal is an awareness of life's energy in all individuals, all things. Their treasure is counted in the synchronicity of an intuitive lifestyle where everything and everyone is present for a purpose—a high purpose that guides and teaches. The multiplication of

these treasures, which James Redfield perceived as flows of sacred energy, transforms the individuals who experience and acknowledge them and, by extrapolation, has the power to transform the planet as human cultures struggle with it today.

Redfield, through *The Celestine Prophecy*, the novel and the movie, is reaching out to the audience. He is counseling us, demonstrating, and perhaps pleading with us to wake up to our potential as sacred expressions of the light and energy that we so casually call "life."

In *The Celestine Prophecy* story, the wisdom contained in the scrolls is about 7,000 years old, but the box buried in the ancient ruins dates from about 1600 A.D. Someone in the early church buried them, perhaps Franciscans inspired by Celestine V. Redfield's point is that Truth cannot be hidden or contained. Truth will surface for those who seek it. Redfield subscribes to the idea that "Hope is Eternal." In his philosophy, the aphorism is not a cliché.

Old Town St. Augustine

*T*he dramatic sequences to be shot in the narrow streets and alleyways of Old Town St. Augustine were scheduled for Thursday and Friday, April 15–16. Wednesday night, director Armand Mastroianni was informed on set that his aged father had died. The news was kept close, and Armand completed the scheduled shooting. The next morning he left to be with his family, and producer/production manager Terry Collis and co-scriptwriter Barnet Bain were called on to direct.

Narrow, cobblestone colonial Aviles Street was transformed by set decorator Vera Mills into a Peruvian marketplace. The transformation of the St. Augustine Old Town shops included Peruvian signage, wall posters, flags, and 11 street vendors, complete with their pushcarts and tables of merchandise that offered fruits and vegetables, bread and pastries, gourds in a cart, Inca Kola, black beans, Indian jewelry, and even soccer balls. Strings

A commemorative sign acknowledges the contribution of the movie to the new Coquina Well Park.

of naked light bulbs above, cane chairs on the sidewalk for the old people, and straw and trash in the street added to the total effect that was then inhabited by a large group of costumed extras who were cast to resemble Peruvians.

With so many merchants, residents, and historic sites involved, local cooperation was essential to obtaining the location. Again, synchronicity seemed to be at work in support of the project. Six months prior to being approached, the neighbors around Aviles Street had formed the Old Town Association; so instead of going from shop to shop and house to house, the location managers could deal with one identity.

Harmony on the Set

During the night filming on streets around the Lightner Museum building, a St. Augustine uniformed police officer was providing traffic control and security. He was curious about the nature of The Celestine Prophecy, and he wanted to know what the film was about. He asked the question because he had worked two previous movie sets where he observed loud arguing and conflict. Since he sensed a calmer, more cooperative environment on The Celestine Prophecy set, he was moved to inquire—why was this movie different from the others? The answer was given as the movie's purpose. He seemed pleased at the response.

What compensation would satisfy the Old Town Association members? Again, their intention was synchronistic to the making of the movie. The Old Town Association had wanted to restore an area on Bravo Lane between Aviles and Charlotte Streets, where the oldest remaining Spanish well in the city was preserved. The site had provided a treasure trove to archaeologists, and now its neighbors wanted to landscape the area around

the historic well as a pocket park where visitors might rest on benches in a quiet spot. Would *The Celestine Prophecy* production company be interested in jump-starting this project with a donation? Enthusiasm on both sides resulted in the establishment of a new landmark in Old Town St. Augustine. Today, the sign commemorating the Coquina Well Park notes the contribution of *The Celestine Prophecy*, the movie.

Producer Barnet Bain consults with Matthew Settle when director Armand Mastroianni is suddenly called away.

Filming the Chase and R*

John (Matthew Settle) flees from the searching National Police.

*I*n the alley behind Wil's Lima apartment, John stumbles in flight from the sirens of a police cruiser that then swings onto the street in search of him. The script reads that an alley door opens, and Wil appears to pull John out of danger. It is their first encounter.

In an alley off Aviles Street, a dark archway is substituted for the door—the location itself dictated the composition of the scene. The director that night had to work out the givens of the location to serve the script and plan the shot on the spot while the company of camera people, electricians, and grips waited for a decision. Script to film is a moment-to-moment process involving change and creative intuition. The pace, however, is very fast, very demanding on everyone involved. Filmmaking is not a job for the indecisive.

SOLA →

cue

Jensen (Jürgen Prochnow) searches the streets for John.

Wil (Thomas Kretschmann) rescues John by taking him off the dangerous streets.

The Ocala Location

The Celestine Prophecy required a remote tropical rainforest with the suggestion of mountains to fulfill the needs of the movie script. Terry Collis's location search led to the potential of deep quarry sites outside Ocala, and the location specialists spent four days hacking their way through dense underbrush to view one limestone quarry after another. Later, the best quarry, which had been dug on a 155-acre site and then abandoned, was viewed by production designer Jim Schoppe and then still later by director Armand Mastroianni, producers-screenwriters James Redfield and Barnet Bain, and executive producer Salle Redfield.

The search and decision process alone had taken seven months, and the second-growth forest had been seen leafless and full, and its 60-foot limestone cliffs seen in dark storms and in bright sunlight. The site also included a lake that arose from the aquifer and a deep cave carved into a steep limestone wall that was full of native bats.

The final negotiation for temporary lease of the quarry location required the filmmakers to build a network of access roads, clean up a massive dumping ground, and erect a high chain-link security fence, but the effort resulted in the use of a magnificent landscape that could not have been manufactured at any affordable price.

On entering the quarry location, a vehicle bumps and jars along on a primitive dirt road and climbs and descends through a dense underbrush and a diffusion of deciduous trees no more than 30 years old. Suddenly, a sheer limestone wall rises from near the road to the height of a six-story building. The wall is gray with hints of ingrained white shell. Once this place was an ocean floor. Then the road is pinched on both sides by the high rock walls, and then it expands into a forest clearing—a man-made oval in the center of a boxed canyon, where trees above on the crest form green leafy umbrellas that filter the sun. Are we in Florida, or in the mountainous forests of Peru?

The job of converting a rainforest quarry landscape into realistic sets for moviemaking was the responsibility of production director Jim Schoppe. His construction crew had two

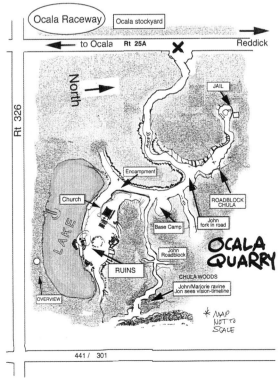

A concept rendering of the church and the outdoor altar

months to construct a rebel prison camp, an authentic seventeenth-century Spanish colonial chapel, and a Mayan temple ruins with a plaza large enough to accommodate battle scenes with mounted conquistadors as well as modern equipped soldiers. The ruins set has many features, including a huge freestanding arch, a ceremonial stone altar, boulders as large as automobiles, a crumbling two-story temple ruins, and a massive line of ancient columns rising out of the middle of the wide crescent-shaped lake that filled the limestone dig with water from the aquifer. All these sets also had to be dressed with foliage to make them appear natural.

In the film, there is a prologue that takes the audience back in time to when a simple rural priest is teaching from the Celestine scrolls at the ruins. Among the gathered peasants are the principal actors Matthew, Thomas, Annabeth, and Sarah Wayne, who will return in modern day as seekers of the lost Insights. Jürgen is also present in the action sequence in his role of denying the spiritual seekers their enlightenment. Are these past-life experiences that we are witnessing? Do true seekers endure and return time after time until the Insights

Celestine Prophecy
the Movie

CELESTINE RUIN
4 SIDED COLUMN
3/3

are understood? As audience, look for the characters behind their beards and period costumes who will make a contemporary quest to regain the lost scrolls.

Back along a crushed limestone road that is littered with brown leaf mulch and torn greenery, a curving lane hacked through the overgrowth continues past a limestone cliff rising like a windowless monolith skyscraper. The steep banks rise from the green fingers of ferns along the path into a tangled woods of white bird and travelers palms, palmetto, Chinese fans, wax myrtle, box elders, and hackberry trees. A long line of five black power cables snakes through the side underbrush to the remote filming site where two men—John and Sanchez—make critical decisions about following their intuition in a dangerous environment. Nearly 30 filmmakers with camera and lights face the actors at the end of the rainforest trail. Behind them, a hundred yards away, the twisted path and the narrow road are empty except for a lone production assistant who sits on a boulder listening through a headset to the first assistant director. Suddenly, the PA shouts to the empty forest road, "Stand by! We're rolling!"

If you stay alert, you notice certain ideas, images, coming to your mind. They're there to guide you. Follow them and the coincidences begin to increase. You step into the flow.

Marjorie (Sarah Wayne Callies) is found by John (Matthew Settle).

John and Marjorie prepare to run free.

Escape from the Jungle Prison

*I*t seems that John, as the seeker of the Insights, is in a life-and-death struggle. The surly sage who warned, "It's a jungle out there," when referring to modern life, was never more correct, but the dangers in the literal jungle are also symbols for an emotional chaos that seems to shadow unfulfilled lives. We all have much to overcome to gain the perspective of insights that will change our attitudes and our circumstances.

Deep in the movie jungle, there is a crude prison camp where John and Marjorie are being held captive. John recognizes the place and the situation from a dream. His intuition subdues his fear, and thus he anticipates the crucial moment of escape when the opportunity presents itself, and he and Marjorie again run free.

John and Marjorie in a power struggle at the crossroads.

When couples first meet, there's usually this wonderful feeling. But it almost never lasts. One person always gets insecure and starts controlling, wanting more of the other's energy. Then the other person feels drained and fights back, and it leads to a power struggle. Every time, every time.

No, it doesn't. If each person stays connected . . . then whoever has the strongest intuition, the best idea, *leads*. There's no competition. The control is shared. That's the kind of relationship I want.

At Miguel's secluded cabin (actually shot at the Washington Oaks location), the Prophecy seekers rendezvous to study the scrolls and to understand their interpersonal relationships. Meanwhile, Wil is having a mysterious encounter with The Little Girl, who keeps appearing to the core group of seekers in their visionary dreams. As John, Marjorie, Father Sanchez, and Julia leave the cabin, The Little Girl appears to them in the flesh and fulfills Julia's persistent longing for the child. In the prologue, envisioned as a past life, Julia and the child were mother and daughter.

But it doesn't
have to be
that way.

At the Cabin

It's the Eighth Insight. Instead of *taking* energy from each other, you *give* it. No matter what.

It's one thing to give energy, but if we give it to someone who is giving it back, then we build up the energy
among ourselves. It amplifies. Back and forth.

Giving is the secret to keeping *yourself* connected. Because the energy, the love, fills you up first as it flows out to others.

*Julia and The Little Girl are seen
as mother and daughter in the prologue.*

At the cabin, the mystical child
reappears and Julia recognizes her.

Jungle Atmosphere

The access roads, now seen as wide, dusty trails canopied by overgrowth, fan out like fingers where the limestone miners have dug deep canyons. On a hot day the remote pathways are cool and shaded. Birds can be heard, and the sound of the massive film company generator is only a distant faint throbbing. Speaking voices do not reach into the recesses, but a shout or a hearty laugh can be heard filtered through veils of green leaves as though they were the end lines of a vibrant poetry. In the stillness, a confident lizard poses on the bent curve of a wild grapevine, and a fly breaks the air with the harshness of rapid wings. A vector of light slides down a limestone wall that resembles the ruins of stucco, and a long, black snake glides across the trail as its witness. Such silence is green and white, not the golden garment of afternoon that drapes itself over stones and wraps itself around the west curve of trees. Human endeavor will shrink from this place one evening sunset with only the sentinels of high rock walls to echo their passing.

En Route to the Ruins

There is a moment in *The Celestine Prophecy* when John is in desperate circumstances, in fear of losing his life, running in a blind panic . . . it is the moment when the mind surrenders, when the ego understands that it has never been in control. In that moment, there is the possibility of understanding for John. In silence, in the release of circumstance and social conditioning, the divine connection is made both possible and self-evident. For John, the ancient adage that the teacher will appear when the student is ready occurs. John's amazing experience is confirmed and explained by Sanchez.

"You opened up. You are changed," Sanchez tells John.

John's transformation has allowed him a glimpse into the future. It has also allowed him to accept that everything that happened in his life prepared him for gaining the Insights. But John is not fully realized yet according to *The Celestine Prophecy* revelations. Sanchez points to the Seventh Insight—the need to discover personal guidance.

"If you stay alert," Sanchez explains, "you notice certain ideas, images, coming to your mind. They're there to guide you. Follow them and the coincidences begin to increase. You step into the flow."

John will come to many forks in the road, literal and figurative, and he must rely on intuition to keep him in the energy flow. He must become aware of the enhanced reality that provides the appropriate direction, a direction that leads to the fulfillment of his destiny.

John's destiny has a synchronistic connection to that of Marjorie, Sanchez, Wil, Julia, and even the destructive Jensen, and the climax of their interconnectedness is driving them ever closer to the Celestine Ruins and the powerful intent of the scrolls themselves.

On one level, we can view the quest for the Insights as an action adventure that involves us and excites us. On a higher level of vibration, however, the allegorical elements of the plot are felt in the subconscious and pose questions that we all must answer for ourselves, sooner or later, after leaving the theater or whenever life seems to be in crisis. We are all connected to the character John in this regard.

Just keep learning, John. You'll find help. There is always help. The right person will come along.

Alone and on the run, John
begins to experience the Insights.

The Bus Explosion

The cast and crew had been working up to one of the film's pyrotechnic extravaganzas—the exploding of the bus, "El Corazon de Perú." For three days with principal actors and about 50 extras and stuntmen, there had been filming around the bus as it was held up by rebels and then attacked by a convoy of heavily armed Peruvian soldiers. The large school-type bus had been painted red, pink, and green and stenciled with stars, hearts, and floral patterns. Its six-stop rural mountain route was hand lettered on both sides above the open

Rebel guerillas attack the bus.

windows. A baggage rack on the back third of the roof showed boxes of produce, battered suitcases, and blankets. Melons, cabbage, corn, and two crates of live chickens (who laid eggs during the filming) were visible.

The day prior to the big explosion, the crew had filmed a soldier firing a bazooka at the bus. Now we would film the result.

Armand directs the bus attack setup with DP Michael Givens from an above-the-treetops crane platform.

The traffic tie-up on the isolated jungle road as the attack begins

SFX coordinator Joe Digaetano and his three SFX technicians had their serious game faces on as they wired the bus with explosive charges and installed bags of gasoline. No one could approach the bus as it was prepared to go hot. The atmosphere on the set changed from jovial to concerned, and those not actively working the scene gathered in small groups down the dusty road and around a curve in the safe zone. Two brave stuntmen, however, were closer so that they could be filmed as bodies flung into the air against the background of the fireball.

All cameras would roll for the exploding bus, and an ambulance with paramedics and the Marion County Fire Department, with a pumper truck, were standing by for added safety. Then the countdown began after repeated warnings of, "Fire in the hole!" Many wore the earplugs that were distributed. The explosion was horrific—more powerful than most people had anticipated. The fireball went up the height of the six-story limestone cliffs, and the shock wave rattled the canyon trees. Out of the yellow shaft of flame, the hood of the bus careened like a flaming meteor and shocked the onlookers as it fell into the woods. The cast and crew waited until the end word "cut" was sounded, and then everyone applauded and cheered.

The fire department moved in to douse the flames, and eventually the "all clear" was given. The assembled company was able to view the destroyed bus and to congratulate those who had made the event so dramatic. Moviemaking is often tedious, but everyone on the set gets their pulse up when the special effects go hot.

Waiting in the hot car, Annabeth Gish relieves the tension by putting her bare foot on Joaquim De Almeida's shoulder.

Marjorie
(Sarah Wayne Callies)
seeks shelter.

John and Father Sanchez escape from the explosion.

THE CELESTINE PROPHECY

OTS DOWN FROM SWORDSMAN
ON HORSE
— ON JOHN AND MARJ   CUT

IN

STUNT SHOT

03

ARM WOUND

SWORD WIPES THRU SHOT   CUT
— NICKED BY SWORD
ANGLE   WOUNDED
ON JOHN   MARJ BACKS AWAY

LOW
ANG.   HE SLUMPS TO GROUND
IN SR - APPARENTLY DEAD
— STARTS TO RUN

In the movie's prologue, a rural parish church, circa 1622, is seen built on the site of a long-lost temple ruins. It is the scene of a brutal attack on the worshipers by mounted conquistadors, and the church is set on fire. On the adjacent lake, Atlantean-styled columns jut out of the water amid the lily pads and support the atmosphere of antiquity.

Filming the Past Lives

When the scenes fast-forward nearly five hundred years to the present day, the partially destroyed church and the temple ruins must be deconstructed, aged, and landscaped to reflect the significant passage of time.

The quest for the Ninth Insight comes full circle back to the temple ruins hidden in the mountainous Peruvian rainforest. This is the ultimate déjà vu for John as the ancient attack on the Insights that he saw in his dreams is repeated by modern soldiers. This, then, is the moment of his truth and the supreme test of his courage and the progress of his spiritual convictions.

The Little Girl
(Rachel Erickson)
escapes with the
scrolls, thus saving
them for the future.

The Choice

Throughout the movie, the character Jensen personifies and represents the worldview that materialistic power, not divine spirituality, is the basis of reality. On first contact, Jensen attempts to control John by fear and offers him safe passage out of the danger zone of revolution. When the promise of security will not dissuade John, Jensen then tries to imprison him and all the seekers of the scrolls until he can destroy the source of their quest—the documented Insights and the ancient ruins from where they came.

Jensen summarized his view by taunting John and saying, "You Americans. So naïve. Thinking there's something spiritual guiding this world. Well, there's nothing out there. Just us humans. And those of us who know that will always be in control. The way of the world is power!"

Jensen, however, does not survive his own evil intents. When he tries to kill John with a combat knife, something goes wrong with the explosive detonators. John saves himself by diving into a dry well that he has seen in a dream. Jensen, who is visionless, dies in the explosion.

Jensen's archetype is evident throughout human history, and James Redfield reminds the audience that humanity keeps repeating its primary error by accepting Jensen's worldview over the spiritual choice. In the film's prologue that keeps coming back to John in flashes of intuitive memory, we clearly see the birthmark on the nobleman's arm that reappears on Jensen's arm. The sign is a confirmation that little has changed in the human struggle over a period of thousands of years. Nevertheless, what John has learned from the Insights alerts him to imminent danger, and he is able to escape Jensen's designs in an explosive climax.

In the end, John, Marjorie, Julia, The Little Girl, and Father Sanchez are made to witness General Martez's spectacular destruction of the Celestine ruins. The giant ruins, the legacy of millennia, is reduced to smoke and rubble. Cardinal Sebastian then takes pity on the party of spiritual revolutionaries and asks General Martez to spare them. "These people can do you no harm now. They'll have no credibility. I'll make sure of it. Let them live. The originals are destroyed. The jungle will take the ruins. Nothing is left of this Prophecy. It's finished."

In the material world, all seems to be lost to the seekers, but what about the truths that they hide in their hearts?

Father Sanchez consoles John about the loss of the scrolls. "They don't matter. We were able to understand the Ninth. We know where we can go if we follow the coincidences. That's the knowledge that will change everything."

On the screen, in the collective experiences of the audience, the corruption of the world seems to offer nothing more than conflict and suffering; and yet within each individual, the real power of the Insights now resides, and if practiced, the result will be a new, transforming personal vision that will ultimately produce a positive worldview.

John escapes the premature detonation of
the explosives by diving into a dry well.

Father Sanchez and John after explosion

Climax at the Ruins

Throughout the movie, John has been in the process of developing an intuitive inner compass. Each individual Insight has proved to be a true direction, and now John arrives at the goal of the Ninth Insight and the climax of the story.

James Redfield believes that John's goal—everyone's goal—is both spiritual and evolutionary and that humanity is headed toward a higher consciousness, a crossing over into a new dimension of daily reality.

In the film's climax, we see John's brief realization of the Ninth Insight as he experiences the higher energy vibration of conscious evolution, and he becomes invisible to the Peruvian soldiers who seek to capture him. In these dramatic moments, the audience witnesses John's gain of the Ninth Insight. Marjorie and Father Sanchez experience it, too, and then Wil, Father José, and a host of Angelic Beings, who have orchestrated the synchronicity of the seekers' lives, come out of the Light to join with them in the sacred dimension. The bliss, however, is short-lived.

John, Marjorie, and Father Sanchez are suddenly aware of the desperate, piercing screams of Julia and The Little Girl as they struggle against the ruthless soldiers. Seeing the cruelty of the soldiers, Marjorie and John allow fear and anger to suppress their energy levels, and they are made visible again. Even Father Sanchez reacts to the implied danger and again becomes a prisoner of the world.

This scene is a profound allegory about the human condition and its experience with higher consciousness and the great mystery of metaphysics. There are moments of great

Sc 117

(FX) ANDES MOUNTAIN PLATE

ON SCE...

THOUSANDS of ANGELIC BEINGS APPEAR FROM THE RUINS AND ACROSS THE LAKE BEYOND- SEEMINGLY INTO INFINITY AS JOHN, WIL, MARJORIE AND JOSE LOOK ON - INTENSE DISTANT LIGHT RADIATES FROM DISTANT CENTER SCREEN .

insights that can transport us into the bliss of a spiritual dimension; but if we allow fear and the resulting anger to dishearten us, we cannot hold on to it. The moment clearly identifies the paradox of spiritual being: How can we be in the world but not of it? How can we live at cause and not become the victims of effect?

John, our protagonist, has literally seen the Light; but now with a knowledge of it, how can he regain that energy and move along its path toward his greater destiny—perhaps to the discovery of a Tenth Insight?

At the end of the movie, John emerges from the National Police headquarters to be reassured by Father Sanchez that all the Celestine seekers have survived. Deported, and on the airplane home, John recognizes a synchronistic message that there is indeed a Tenth Insight. The adventure of life continues.

The Guidance within evolves the world toward a heaven that is already here. To know this is to know our destiny.

(FX)

ANDES MOUNTAIN PLATE

WIDE ON SCENE

- **THOUSANDS** OF ANGELIC BEINGS APPE
FROM THE RUINS AND ACROSS THE LAKE
SEEMINGLY INTO INFINITY AS JOHN, W
- INTENSE DISTANT LIGHT RADIATES
CENTER SCREEN.

SC117

18 RUINS

WIDE ANGLE ON SOUTH RUINS.
ETHERIAL BEINGS APPEAR- EMERGING FROM RUINS
* GLOW FROM OS

JOHN (OC): THEY'RE ALL HELPING...

GLOW

We're being shown Heaven. It's not
somewhere else. It's right here.

It's where evolution has always been
trying to take us. That's the Ninth Insight.

When the enlightened ones react to the recapture of Julia and The Little Girl, however, and fear is allowed to reappear, so do they, and they are also captured.

En route home, John is aware of a synchronistic message that leads him to believe that there is indeed a Tenth Insight.

The cardinal intercedes for the captives and prevents them from being killed.

Maysie Hoy — A.C.E. Editor

Maysie Hoy read *The Celestine Prophecy* when it first appeared and found it very synergistic with her own beliefs. She feels that editing this movie is important work on multiple levels.

Maysie began in films as an actress and got her first credit on Robert Altman's *McCabe and Mrs. Miller*. For the next eight years, she worked with Altman on *California Split*, *Nashville*, and *Three Women and a Wedding*, and by the filming of Altman's *Buffalo Bill and the Indians*, she had moved into the sound and editing departments. Maysie was one of the earliest members of the American Film Institute's Directing Women's Workshop. She serves on the board of directors of the Motion Picture Editors Guild, has been a faculty member of the Los Angeles Film School, and was featured as one of 30 actors and craftswomen honored in the book *Great Women of Film.*

Maysie likes to key on the sounds of an actor speaking or on the soundtrack of a visual effect when she edits. She is looking and listening to establish a rhythm in the flow of the storytelling. In a key scene between Wil and the mystical child, where they increase their combined energies to create a spiritual glow, Maysie has the wondrous metaphysical event described by Julia in an overvoice from the preceding cabin scene where she is describing the Eighth Insight to John. Instead of cross-cutting the two separate events, Maysie unites them with a sensitive edit.

Editor Maysie Hoy with James Redfield in the editing suite

Maysie also has the *What Dreams May Come* connection to producers Barnet Bain and Terry Collis. She was the co-editor of that award-winning film. Other memorable films that she has edited include *The Joy Luck Club* (her first major credit) and *Smoke*, a Harvey Keitel classic.

Producers Terry and Barnet

Bobbie Collis, production coordinator

Dave Jackson, assistant editor;
and Brian Beard,
post production assistant and
personal assistant to Terry Collis

John Howard,
post production
supervisor

Glenn Nicol,
accountant

Visual Effects — Post Production
John Nugent/Nick Brooks

John Nugent and Nick Brooks with director Armand
Mastroianni on location in the Cloud Forest of Costa Rica

Visual effects in moviemaking are equal parts fine artistry and technical wizardry. A fine arts painter may be able to render a dramatic tableau on canvas, but can he or she reproduce it at the digital workstation? Up until recent times, there was no film school for visual effects technicians. Those driven to work in the technological age of this art form had to learn it from the pioneers who had preceded them in the process of countless digital software experiments that produced the closely guarded "black art tricks." And most of the visual effects trade is still pure dimensional magic.

The making of *The Celestine Prophecy* movie required exceptional sensitivity to the sequences in which spiritual epiphanies are realized by the characters on screen. The assignment went to an award-winning visual effects team led by John P. Nugent, supervisor, and Nick Brooks, consultant. John Nugent refers to Nick Brooks as his visual effects mentor. Nick brought John onto the *What Dreams May Come* team, and then the following year onto *The Matrix* team. John then relocated his family to New Zealand for three years to work on *The Lord of the Rings* trilogy. As the visual effects department head, John supervised over 150 artists in creating one of the most wondrous visual extravaganzas in motion picture history.

Nick Brooks has more than 25 feature film credits as a visual effects supervisor or consultant. In 1998, Nick won the Academy Award for the visual effects of "the painted world" in *What Dreams May Come*, a film produced by Barnet Bain. His credits include *Eraser*, *The Matrix*, *Blade II*, and *Dreamkeeper*, an ABC miniseries for which he won an Emmy Award.

In post-production, the job of the visual effects artists on *The Celestine Prophecy* was to faithfully render the images that James Redfield had so strikingly described in the novel. James, of course, had his own ideas of what these images should look like in the film, but so did millions of his readers. Somehow, in the initial scenes of Julia observing John and Marjorie exchanging energy in the Viciente garden, the visual effects had to meet the expectations of the audience. The visual effects not only had to be believable, but they also had to be seamless as pieces of artistic cinematic storytelling. Late in the movie, when the host of angelic beings emerges out of the light in the climactic Celestine ruin scenes, the audience should experience the same wondrous, emotional awe that the central characters feel on the screen. To make the spiritual revelations of *The Celestine Prophecy* available to theater audiences thus required unique artistic and technical talents as well as the ability to share the novel's original vision. For this process, the visual effects digital artists had the participation of James Redfield himself. From Studio City, California, to a digital studio in western Massachusetts, James was there to coax the images of his imagination onto film.

Nuno Malo
Composer

Celestine composer Nuno Malo with his
wife, pianist Ivana Grubelic Malo

Nuno Malo's mother encouraged him to read *The Celestine Prophecy* in his native Portugal. Ten years later, with a master's degree in composing from the London College of Music, post-graduate studies in scoring for motion pictures at USC, and the ASCAP Film Scoring Workshop in Los Angeles, Nuno learned that the book that had been so important to his family was now a feature film in production.

Nuno, only 26 years old at the time, had ample credits and musical scoring examples to share in his audition CD. He had scored three features produced in Portugal—*Manô, Fado Blues* with a soundtrack CD, and *Police Woman*, a film that had appeared at festivals worldwide. In addition, his solo CD *Star-Crossing* had been nominated as Best Instrumental Album at the Golden Melody Awards, Asia's top talent showcase.

After his initial demo CD was heard, Nuno was invited to submit a second CD of original thematic music appropriate to *The Celestine Prophecy;* and although many other composers were heard, the producers kept coming back to Nuno. Some of the original melodies in the second CD remain in the final score. After only four years in Hollywood, Nuno found himself collaborating with the author of one of his most esteemed books; and during the scoring process, James Redfield was an almost daily visitor to his studio. Nuno felt that he was experiencing the true meaning of synchronicity.

The Northwest Sinfonia and Chorale, conducted by Joe Crnko, performing the Celestine score in the Bastyr University Chapel north of Seattle

*Music scoring mixer
Robert Fernandez discussing the
score with composer Nuno Malo*

Nuno's musical connections extend to the Budapest Symphony Orchestra in Hungary, the Bulgarian Symphony Orchestra in Sofia, and the Radio Slovak Symphony Orchestra in Slovakia, but the movie music was ultimately performed in Seattle, Washington, by the Northwest Sinfonia and Chorale, with Joe Crnko conducting.

Still Photography
Jon Farmer

Jon Farmer began his photographic career studying with such notable fine arts photographers as Wynn Bullock, Clarence John Laughlin, and Ansel Adams. His photographs were featured in the book *New American Nudes* and in the Martin Scorsese film *New York Stories*. Jon also photographed the American and European tours

for the famed Louis Falco Modern Dance Company. His fine art photography is centered on spiritual and mystical themes and has been featured in solo and group exhibitions at museums and galleries all over the United States.

As a still photographer on motion picture sets, Jon has worked for all the major Hollywood studios and photographed many leading actors, including Sean Connery, Will Smith, Sean Penn, Jude Law, Sandra Bullock, and Melanie Griffith.

Jon's extensive feature film credits show a great deal of diversity. Examples include *All the King's Men*, *Wild Things*, *Bad Boys*, *Ace Ventura: Pet Detective*, and *My Girl*.

Jon was drawn to photograph *The Celestine Prophecy* because of his personal synchronicity with its spiritual and transcendent themes.

*Jon Farmer (left) with movie book
co-author and photo editor Monty Joynes*

Monty Joynes, who wrote the narrative and edited this movie book, is best known for his four novels in the Booker Series (*Naked into the Night*, *Lost in Las Vegas*, *Save the Good Seed*, and *Dead Water Rites*), which deals with Anglo entry into the culture and metaphysics of contemporary American Indians. Monty has written and edited professionally in magazine and book publishing for more than 35 years. He also has writer-director credits in two short films.

Additional Still Photo Credits

All photographs by Jon Farmer except those noted on the following pages.
Film frames by cinematographer Michael Givens.

Nathanael J. Murray, moviebook liaison and personal assistant to producer Barnet Bain

The Celestine Prophecy: The Movie

Main Titles

A Celestine Films and Barnet Bain Production
In Association with the Kingston Companies

The Celestine Prophecy

Matthew Settle
Thomas Kretschmann
Sarah Wayne Callies
Annabeth Gish
Obba Babatunde
Robyn Cohen
John Aylward
Castulo Guerra
with Hector Elizondo
with Joaquim De Almeida
and Jürgen Prochnow as Jensen
Casting Director: Andrea Stone, C.S.A.
Production Designer: James L. Schoppe
Original Music: Nuno Malo
Film Editing: Maysie Hoy, A.C.E. and Scott Vickrey, A.C.E.
Director of Photography: R. Michael Givens
Executive Producer: Salle Merrill Redfield
Producers: Barnet Bain, Terry Collis, James Redfield, and Beverly Camhe
Based on the novel by James Redfield
Screenplay by James Redfield and Barnet Bain
Directed by Armand Mastroianni

Hampton Roads Publishing Company publishes books on a variety of subjects, including metaphysics, spirituality, health, visionary fiction, and other related topics.

We also create on-line courses and sponsor an *Applied Learning Series* of author workshops. For a current list of what is available, go to www.hrpub.com or request the ALS workshop catalog at our toll-free number.

For a copy of our latest trade catalog, call toll-free, 800-766-8009, or send your name and address to:

HAMPTON ROADS PUBLISHING COMPANY, INC.
1125 STONEY RIDGE ROAD CHARLOTTESVILLE, VA 22902
E-mail: hrpc@hrpub.com Internet: www.hrpub.com